Structures in Beckett's *Watt*

Dedication

Ai miei cari genitori con cui vorrei scambiar vita per rivederli ringiovaniti, e a Franca e agli altri membri della mia cara famiglia i cui sacrifici, le speranze, l'orgoglio mi hanno dato forza attraverso gli anni, questo libro rappresenta poco più che nulla.

To my dear parents whose life together I wish I could exchange with mine only to see them young again, and to Fran and the other members of my family whose sacrifices, hopes, and pride have always given me heart, this fruit is little acknowledgment of their worth.

Structures in Beckett's *Watt*

by

John C. Di Pierro

French Literature Publications Company
York, South Carolina
1981

Get the nothingness back into words. The aim is words with nothing to them; words that point beyond themselves rather than to themselves; transparencies, empty words. Empty words, corresponding to the void in things.

Norman O. Brown, *Love's Body*

The form itself becomes a preoccupation, because it exists as a problem separate from the material it accommodates. To find a form that accommodates the mess, that is the task of the artist now.

Samuel Beckett

To know nothing, is nothing, not to want to know anything likewise, but to be beyond knowing anything, that is when peace enters in, to the soul of the incurious seeker.

Samuel Beckett

All is possible.

Samuel Beckett, *Watt*

Preface

John DiPierro has chosen one of the most recondite, most promising, and least yielding of Beckett's novels to study. It has become customary among critics faced with a Beckett novel, to describe it in terms of other things, poetic-psychic analogues—crosses, circles, chinese puzzles, and centaurs. DiPierro is no exception. If I may join the game, *Watt* recalls a visit I made a few years ago to a restaurant in a French town in the provinces. In the rear of the restaurant was a door clearly marked *W. C.* Upon opening it, expecting to find nothing other than a toilet, I looked out onto the alley one floor below.

Watt is like that. It is a closed house with a 1000 doors. It invites us to walk in, but when we enter one of the doors we find ourselves on the outside.

Among modern novelists, Beckett's conscious manipulation of form and language establishes him among the descendency of Marcel Proust, Dorothy Richardson and James Joyce (no one so much as the last), while his predilection for philosophic speculation owes itself to diverse currents running through the pre-Socratics, Giordano Bruno, Vico, and Hegel. The coincidence of the two lines results in a supreme novelistic example of the formalist-metaphysical writer of the twentieth century.

To assign Beckett such a category, however, while suggesting to us that he is indeed a novelist's novelist, and that his appeal is to a hardcore intellectual elite, intimates nothing of the reason why his work enchants the faithful like a serpent's eye nor why his novels are unsurpassed in speaking to us of the post-Einsteinian world of the present age.

If Beckett is a novelist's novelist, *Watt* is a novel's novel. How do we cope with it? The only way to enter it is simultaneously, through all its many doors. DiPierro tries exactly that. The reason Beckett's critics, in speaking of *Watt*, speak of it analogically, is precisely because Beckett's novels, unlike traditional narrative, are not *about* anything. They *are*. Beckett, in his essay on "Dante . . . Bruno. Vico . . . Joyce," says of Joyce's work: "This writing is not *about* something; *it is that something itself.*" Accordingly, DiPierro asserts, "The meaning of the work of art is the meaning of its form." He thereupon undertakes to develop a comprehensive view of the intergral unity of *Watt's* structures.

The problem Beckett has set up for himself in *Watt*, as in all of his work, has been, as DiPierro emphasizes, to find a way of structuring unstructurable phenomena which constitute what we contentedly call "reality." The enormity of his task, taken up time and again, and leading us ever more into silence and stasis, suggests that he has failed in terms of his ability to structure reality into something knowable. But DiPierro proposes, as some critics have before him, that through its very structural convulsions *Watt* transforms itself into a formal metaphor that accommodates the formlessness of life. To achieve that metaphor, there has to occur an apotheosis by which the novel becomes more than its parts. DiPierro attempts ultimately, by entering one by one the manifold entryways of *Watt*, to show us how, by simultaneous ingress, we may truly find ourselves *within* the house.

Does he succeed? I think he does, to the degree that it can be done. The problem of the critic parallels the problem that confronted Beckett himself. DiPierro does not in the end reveal what the novel is about, for that would be to reveal what Beckett himself was unable to reveal—the formlessness of life. DiPierro does, on the other hand, show us how the diverse structures in Beckett's novel function, how they interact in order to bring about something greater than themselves—what Edgar Roberts (cited by DiPierro) calls "a total impression," or what Piaget calls "over-all properties distinct from the properties of its [the structure's] elements" (also cited by DiPierro).

So our critic pursues the task of examining the "syntactic, semantic, and verbal structures" of *Watt,* their interrelationships and "synthesis in the total structure of the work." In his tri-partite exploration, he first looks at "character," more in its fifteenth-century sense of "graphic symbol" than in its current literary sense (the Greek *kharaktér* was an "instrument for marking, impress, distinctive nature," according to the *OED*).

While vaguely resembling "characters" in a modern sense, the "graphic symbols" designated Watt, Arsene, Knott, etc., are viewed more profitably by DiPierro as formal verbal configurations (an "exteriorisation of thoughts," as Beckett termed it in his critical essay on Joyce). Little by little, he shows how the "characters" become fleshed out through linguistic accretion (onomastic properties, etymologies, language and anti-language patterns), as well as through their interrelationships. He traces their evolution in terms of a Hegelian dialectic that ends with their transformation into a super-character that dissolves, so the process may begin all over again. Finally, at the end of his chapter on character, DiPierro gathers all the strands in order to explore the "conceptual implications" of the characters and their relationships.

I should like to pause here to make an observation regarding DiPierro's procedure. It becomes increasingly evident as the reader follows the critic's argument that, the way Beckett has built up his characters through slow accretion of characteristics, manifested on discrete, infinitely subtle levels, is the very way the critic himself proceeds.

That approach is perhaps the most original aspect of this study. Which brings us back to a passing remark made early in the introduction when DiPierro refers to George Szanto's *Narrative Consciousness:* "The reader's mind must coincide with the narrator's in order to comprehend and create each form and pattern." That is precisely what DiPierro does. It strikes me that he "reads" Beckett as Beckett might if he were so disposed. It resembles the way Beckett read Joyce.

In other places, DiPierro refers to the helplessness of traditional analytic modes in confronting Beckett's novel. *Watt* is relatively impervious to *explication de texte* because, to explicate a text, we need a context, and it is nearly impossible to establish a coherent context. Catch-22 in an earlier version. It is furthermore meaningless to isolate fragments of Beckett's novels to discuss because what we end up with is precisely what we began with, isolated fragments.

If DiPierro teaches us anything, it is perhaps foremost how to read a Beckett novel. We have to go for the whole thing. *Watt* has to be consumed whole, regurgitated, and consumed again. Not until then can we be satisfied that we have feasted with the Romans. To mix metaphors, gem-like *précis* torn from the flesh of Beckett's work will simply not do. The glitter of the work may be there, but the crown jewels are missing.

Perhaps DiPierro points a method and a way that will bring us closer to Beckett's work, a rare type of assimilative reading which goes back over the work by re-creating it—not as Blanchot does to Kafka, into a new creation, but as a recovery process of the original creation. Though DiPierro refers to some structuralist critics and uses some of their vocabulary, his reading is unorthodox structuralist. At the same time, it may be more fundamentally structuralist than that of many of the orthodox structuralists who say the right things, awe us by brilliant *aperçus*, but leave us hanging in mid-air. Aside from being a type of assimiliative analysis, DiPierro's study is holistic. The result averts the danger Beckett himself warned against, that of "the neatness of identification."

William Blake said, "If the doors of perception were cleansed everything would appear to man as it is, infinite." However we play on the image of doors, we unarguably come closer in the present study to entering Beckett's *Watt* and seeing it "as it is, infinite." In the remarkable book *Doors of Perception,* which takes Blake's words for its title, Aldous Huxley describes his experience with mescaline in the following way. "Place and distance cease to be of much interest. The mind does its perceiving in terms of intensity of existence, profundity of significance, relationships within a pattern." I hardly wish to suggest that mescaline had anything to do with Beckett's novel or DiPierro's study, but the *way* we perceive *Watt* spells the difference between banging against a blank wall and undergoing the profound experience that Tzara called the "infinite and shapeless variation" of existence.

To return to DiPierro's study, the chapter following fastens on plot. Again the conventional acceptances of the term hardly prepare us for *Watt*'s "plot." We come to understand why, though DiPierro speaks of semantic structure, a separate chapter on "meaning" would be meaningless, for meaning inheres in Beckett's form. To cite one example, the critic's observation that, "By showing us how and why *Watt* is going mad the linear sequential structure faces collapse," could just as easily be reversed: the threatened collapse of the linear sequential structure indicates Watt's onset of madness. If we replace Lévi-Strauss' "mythical" structures by the word "formal," we can say that Beckett's formal configurations in *Watt* provide *imagines mundi* that "facilitate an understanding of the world in as much as they resemble it" (Lévi-Strauss, "History and Dialectic"). What is important to understand is that Beckett's thought process works by analogy in the same way that that of "primitive" mythmakers does.

Even as truistic as the idea of the inseparability of form and content has become, most readers continue to separate the two and thereby find Balzac's *La Cousine Bette* (or Guy des Cars' recent *Le Château du Clown*) a much more entertaining novel than *Watt*. Entertainment is not at stake here, however; it is only a by-product of understanding that makes *Watt* tick. Beckett's novel throws up endless barriers in the way of reading for content alone. *Watt*'s "profundity of significance," to use Huxley's term, lies in the experience of existence through its structure, not through some encapsulated "meaning" of it.

The geometric figure DiPierro sees as most important in *Watt*— the circle—signifies more than a device of structuring; it signifies, as he says, "an expression of Beckett's point of view which constantly forms the structure while being formed by it." Like the broken circle in Erskine's room, however, it cannot encompass completely and the break in its circumference is a paradigm of chaos. "Form rules chaos but chaos also rules form."

In his conclusion, DiPierro places *Watt* in the Beckettian novel-istic succession. Beginning with the conventional (if quirky) *Murphy*, it is indeed quite a leap to the crazyquilt structure of *Watt*. But we approach an understanding of how Beckett made this leap after read-ing DiPierro's chapter on "Philosophical and Aesthetic Concepts." He looks at several influences on Beckett's thought, but none so inter-esting (and so neglected) as that of Vico's theory of historical cycles.

With a mind to Beckett's early critical-theoretical writings, his attraction to mantic writing, the short-lived movement of Verticalism, and such novelistic models as Joyce's *Finnegans Wake*, DiPierro offers an informed view of the creative frame of mind Beckett had reached at the time he wrote *Watt*.

In his discussion of modern science, which has turned away from the rational certitude of Cartesian thought, DiPierro shows us how literary creation for someone as finely tuned into his times as Beckett (he had read deeply in mathematics, physics and astronomy) can mirror the most advanced thinking in scientific fields.

Bombarded from all sides by these currents of philosophic and aesthetic speculation, after assimilating them Beckett still faced the problem of casting them into novelistic form. DiPierro seeks in Beckett's real-life situation the events that may have helped to spur him on to create a novel representing such a dramatic formal break with *Murphy*. DiPierro sees in *Watt* a reflection—beyond that of the physical-spiritual properties of life itself—of the political and social madhouse of a Europe at war (*Watt* was composed during the period 1944-1945).

Like many other writers living in France at that time, Beckett led a multi-faceted existence. Just as we sense in Camus' *La Peste* the obsessions brought about by war and realize that without the exile and duplicity inherent in Camus' wartime situation that his novel would undoubtedly have been quite different had it been written at the time of *L'Etranger*, so does the war play a plausible role in the creation of Beckett's *Watt*. But even beyond the French writers of the time who were forced into subterfuge and deceit, to switch masks as the moment called for, Beckett's situation as an Anglo-Irish expatriate compounded the multiplicity of roles and relates no doubt to his multiple personae in *Watt.*

Watt, seen in this way, joins some of the best European "war novels" of the period which, while not treating war at all, are faithful reflections of its pervasive fatalism. To use DiPierro's term to characterize such novels, they treat the "disintegration of the 'I,' " as well as the breakdown of rationalistic systems. Of course, such a subject, as DiPierro himself acknowledges, belongs to another book. But the book we have opened here does indicate to us the reflection in *Watt* of the psycho-literary torment of its author writing at such a time.

As the result in part of these several influences, and perhaps Beckett's own search for aesthetic-personal salvation, *Watt* represents the existence of order within chaos. Several readers and critics, intrigued by the sense of a hidden order governing the disparate parts of the novel, have, after fruitless search, come to the despairing conclusion that *Watt* is a chaotic failure. But DiPierro, in his persistent attempt to "read" *Watt* for what it *is* rather than what it is *about,* brings us a long way along the path (prepared by a few excellent critics before him) in coming to terms with *Watt.*

I believe that many of us, who have experienced a literary lover's quarrel with Beckett's *Watt,* lured by its brilliant writing but frustrated by its seeming inpregnability, can, after reading the present book go back to *Watt* with more promising prospects of reconciliation. Reconciliation with *Watt* demands the process of learning how to "read" in a way unconventional for most readers; it demands a liberation from the rigid expectances of outmoded conventions. If we achieve that, we will learn how to read a novel extraordinarily of our times (or at least of the most advanced thinking of our times).

Sir Richard Steele once said of his wife, "to love her was a liberal education." Love of a good book can equally be a liberal education. And John DiPierro's study goes a long way in helping us resolve our lover's quarrel with a good book.

John D. Erickson

Table of Contents

xvi   *Contents*

Chapter I

Introduction

The purpose of this study is to examine how Beckett has organized the subtle, intricate, kaleidoscopically structured elements that compose his *récit, Watt.* We will take into account all of the discrete yet interdependent components of narrative: the semantic, the verbal, and the syntactic, and their interrelationships that create the unified gestalt of *Watt,* Beckett's neglected masterpiece whose structural subtleties have eluded many of its critics. *Watt* is a multiform novel, one of modified patterns whose dynamic coordinates interconnect and complement one another to provide a vision of the universe which is both multiple and unified.

Beckett revealed his predilection for conscious form in a personal chronicle:

> I take no sides. I am interested in the shape of ideas. There is a wonderful sentence in Augustine: 'do not despair; one of the thieves was saved. Do not presume; one of the thieves was damned.' That sentence has a wonderful shape. It is the shape that matters.[1]

Ever since his 1949 dialogues with Georges Duthuit,[2] Beckett has expounded his concern with form, specifically with the potential forms of expression. He stated on numerous occasions since then that the role of the modern artist is to superimpose artistic order and structure on the formless and chaotic flow of life. There must be a continual movement of text which, though it may seem to violate traditional form and movement, not only preserves art but also widens its possibilities. Beckett's fiction, as he explains twelve years later in an interview with Tom F. Driver, further emphasizes the interdependence of meaning and form and the coexistence in art of confusion and order:

> What I am saying does not mean that there will henceforth be no form in art. It only means that there will be new form and that this form will be of such a type that it admits the chaos and does not try to say that the chaos is really something else. The form and the chaos remain separate. The latter is not reduced to the former. That is why the form itself becomes a preoccupation, because it exists as a problem separate from the material it accommodates. To find a form that accommodates the mess, that is the task of the artist now.[3]

The novelist orders the chaos of his universe through fictional form, and Beckett recognizes the difficulty of the task of structuring elusive reality. Like the enigmatic painting in Erskine's room, reproduced on the cover of the Grove Press edition of *Watt,* life must remain a puzzle. The incomplete circle does not change its nature or become more decipherable to the reader, no matter from how many angles Watt views it.

Watt appears to be a novel of failure—Watt's, Beckett's, Everyman's—to find absolute truth and knowledge. In the Duthuit dialogues, Beckett credits the painter Bram van Velde with being the "first to admit that to be an artist is to fail . . . that failure is his world and to shrink from it desertion . . . . "[4] The artist's task is to think, speak, write, exorcise, and fail, continually and inevitably. The act of writing is essentially one of lying, of endless hypothesizing about the incomprehensible, alien, and chaotic universe—to describe the impossibility of describing life.

One must remember, however, that Beckett's "failure" is essentially epistemological. He does not claim to be the first to deal with what the Pre-Socratics referred to as the surd, the irreducible. For that reason, the multiple structural elements of *Watt* satirically mirror the formless flow of life, symbolized by Knott's chaotic household, a menage which Watt desperately tries to understand. Watt's quest is doomed to failure, ending ultimately in disintegrated speech and deteriorated character.

If Beckett was the first to admit defeat in the face of the imponderable, he was also one of the first artists to reshape the modern novel by creating a new form which accommodated formlessness. This form is built upon patterns and variations which reach something of an apotheosis in *Watt*. There is ironic success in Beckett's art, for it shapes thoughts out of formless matter. Basically an ironist, Beckett laughs sardonically at the task before him—to express the inexpressible. He doubts the worth of words, of conventions, of the mind, yet it is through his masterful manipulation of these elements that he proves his superior creative ability.

Watt is a combination of mutilated elements dispersed in a chaotic form, expressed in rich style and complex, multiple structures with a balance which can be understood only by careful analysis. The meaning of the work of art is the meaning of its form. An appreciation of the art of *Watt* and its subtle, enigmatic patterns depends upon our discerning the modes of representation of this novel. Its structural achievement will be measured not by the movement toward classical purity but by the subtle integration of its disparate elements.

A first reading of *Watt* gives one the impression that its parts do not grow together or develop by logical links with each other. The structure seems to be conceived with no concern for logically developed causation or for the dynamic interaction of the compositional elements of the narrative. A close examination, however, shows each distinct structural element fused together to create a single, unified view of the universe. The composite elements of *Watt* form a tightly and deftly woven web of intricately-related, discrete parts contrapuntally structured around one cohesive unity. The concept of modified patterns clustered around the thematic, verbal, and syntactic variations of Beckett's work should not be rigidly superimposed upon *Watt*, but they should be used as a lens through which the total narrative structure of *Watt* can be perceived.

The bulk of critical material published on *Watt* and on Beckett's work in general has limited itself almost exclusively to Beckett as a thinker rather than as a writer and a craftsman. These critics have contented themselves with commenting upon the novel's themes, and imposing on it traditional slice-of-life concepts. But what is ever-lastingly of value is the inner life of the work, its body chemistry, its form, and its structure; and it is that which will be considered here.

There are, however, a number of notable critics who have taken a more than perfunctory look at *Watt*'s elusive, highly intricate, and sophisticated structures. Hugh Kenner, David Hesla, Raymond Federman, Edith Kern, Ruby Cohn, George Szanto, G. C. Barnard, and Guy Croussy all remark on the overriding unity of the novel despite its multiple, chaotic elements which crumble to nothing, awaiting ultimate silence and the symbolic death of literature.

Kenner points to the symmetries and recurrences observable in the novel and he has also made an exhaustive study of Beckett's themes. His point of departure for his perspicacious thematic study is his reference to Beckett's typical hero as the "Cartesian Centaur." Other critics who have stressed Watt's Cartesianism are Frederick Hoffman, Nathan Scott, Jacqueline Hoefer, and Ruby Cohn. In general, they all see Watt satirically as a Western rationalistic, positivistic, solipsistic robot, a bearer of the Cartesian cross.

Hesla analyzes the relationship between form and chaos. Chaos is synonymous with the absurd which *Watt*'s form must accommodate. Form and chaos remain separate in *Watt,* contraries and oppositions are unresolved. Hesla evaluates Beckett's art as ontological, focusing on man, existence, and the question of identity. However, his critical emphasis is on the writers and philosophers–mainly the Pre-Socratics, Hegel, Kierkegaard, Sartre—who have shaped Beckett's mind. Although he shows some concern with form, Hesla's interpretation is limited primarily to ideas.

Federman comments on the imperfect shape of *Watt* despite its subtly controlled form. He sees the novel's circular plot as extending "backward beyond the beginning of Watt's adventures to relate thematically with the works that precede, and projects forward to prepare the shape of the works to come."[5] Although incomplete, Federman's work is particularly significant in his analysis of the interrelationships among the various structural components. *Watt* is viewed as a satire on philosophy as well as an ironic reflection upon the futility of the creative act. The novel's form for Federman is thus inadequate to provide an understanding of reality.

Kern compares the structure of *Watt* to a Chinese puzzle in its intricacy and delicacy. The formal structure of the novel reflects the Beckettian universe of uncertainty and elusiveness. Cohn stresses the relationship between characterization and theme, viewing *Watt* as a comic novel of failure. According to her, *Watt* is essentially a plotless, multi-perspective work which broadens the concept of situation while narrowing the concept of character.

In Cohn's view there is only one major character in the novel: Watt. He is an atypical hero, lacking character and obsessed with logic, science, and rationality in an irrational world. This incongruity of both Watt and the world is described in terms of the open circle with its dot. Comic emphasis falls upon the circle as a perfect solipsistic symbol, for Watt's circle is also broken. The absurdity of situation and character is stressed: human frailty is flung in the face of mysterious forces.

Szanto's *Narrative Consciousness*[6] traces patterns of relationships among all the structural components of *Watt*. Modified patterns appear through the shifting narrative consciousness of the novel—patterns which permeate the entire composition. The reader's mind must coincide with the narrator's, in order to comprehend and create each form and pattern. This narrative consciousness uses description to bring order out of chaos. The characters' experiences in *Watt* form a series of patterns or one ritualistic central pattern.

Barnard also examines the interrelationships among *Watt*'s compositional elements. He closely examines the characterization and the part that schizophrenia plays in plot and setting as well as characterization in *Watt* and in Beckett's work in general. According to Barnard, an interior sequence rather than the compositional order constitutes the saga of the schizophrenic in Beckett's fiction.

Croussy sees all Beckettian heroes as only one protagonist whose characterization evolves and establishes a line of continuity throughout the author's fiction. Croussy emphasizes theme and characterization as a means of placing *Watt* in the mainstream of Beckett's fiction. In fact, many critics, especially the French, have a predilection for analyzing *Watt* in the light of Beckett's *œuvre*.

As previously noted, many critics devote themselves primarily to thematic studies. John Fletcher's two books provide a great deal of information on *Watt*'s themes of alienation, dualism of mind and body, exile, sexual unease, and, most importantly, the impossibility of gaining any sort of knowledge. Richard Coe finds that many of *Watt*'s themes parallel Proustian themes. He equates the search for self with a circle seeking a center, a center that never can be reached despite endlessly decreasing circles that lead nowhere.

Josephine Jacobsen and William Mueller stress the themes of nothingness, the hypothetical imperative, the quest, and absurdity. Lawrence Harvey, Jean Onimus, Olga Bernal, and David Hesla all discuss *Watt*'s religious themes, underlining the symbolic presence of God in the character of Knott.

William York Tindall stresses the themes of doubt, the unknown, and the unknowable and the unreliability of the narrator. He views Knott's house as being pre-established and arbitrary, indicative of the order and meaning which elude *Watt*. Ihab Hassan considers *Watt* to be a parody of the pretentious rhetoric and delusive logic of conventional philosophy. He believes that the symbolic structure of *Watt* remains quite indefinite, allowing the identification of Watt with Knott and with Christ.

Emphasis has also been placed on Watt's language by many critics. In most cases language is treated as a compositional element, linked correlatively with theme and character. Fletcher, for example, sees a parallel between Watt's mental-physical deterioration and the disintegration of his speech. Federman views language as an ineffective tool of communication. He explains Watt's deterioration from the standpoint of his inability to distinguish reality from illusion.

According to Jacobsen and Mueller in *The Testament of Samuel Beckett*,[7] Beckett's language serves every nuance with marvelous accuracy. They dwell on Watt's linguistic acrobatics, linking them with the theme of the impossibility of acquiring absolute knowledge. In the introduction to his collection of essays on Beckett, Martin Esslin elaborates on the inadequacy of speech and its concomitant ironic success: "Never in fiction, have so many words been used as by Beckett to underline the inefficiency of language and never, by his very language, has anyone disproved the point so brilliantly."[8]

Tindall correlates the permutation in *Watt* with the themes of the unknown and the unknowable: "The serial permutations that make this story tiresome and hilarious are a picture not only of man's mind attempting the unthinkable, but of man's unspeakable life."[9] Hassan considers language a dead habit from which all Beckett's characters suffer, especially Molloy who says: "To restore silence is the role of objects."[10] Objects are thus no more meaningful than the words describing them which they cannot resist. Language seeks its own destruction; no longer capable of expressing thought, it is reduced to metaphoric death: silence.

Kern shares Hassan's views on the inadequacy of language, underlining the connection between the kaleidoscopic nature of language, the elusiveness of truth, and *Watt*'s questionable narration. Richard Coe emphasizes the arbitrariness of language and its relationship to the phenomena it tries to describe. Watt equates words with meanings, using words as an exorcistic release. If we have a name for a thing, "it exists for us and we are safe .... For Watt words and meanings are identical."[11]

Hoffman interprets *Watt* as a testimony to language and the comedy of the impulsive act of speaking. He sees a correlation between language and characterization: in trying to define himself, Watt creates Knott so that he may justify himself by serving Knott. Kenner sees the limitations of language as a conveyor of meaning or a captor of reality. Although Beckettian sentences clearly have a shape, they do not have meaning: "Terms have sounds but not referents, sentences shape but not purport."[12] Cohn stresses Beckett's anti-language techniques in *Watt* by underscoring the inversion of letters in words, words in sentences, sentences in paragraphs. These linguistic inversions are a comic device to show the confusion of Watt's mind and the fact that knowledge lies beyond language.

The French critics generally speak about the language of *Watt* in terms of stylistics and thematics. In her *Langage et fiction dans le roman de Beckett,*[13] Olga Bernal discusses Watt's experiences with words and language, equating Watt's deteriorating character with his disintegration of speech. The meaninglessness and unintelligibility of the universe is a thematic correlative of language and characterization. Janvier stresses the use of repetition and puns for comic effect and he looks at Beckett's types of language.

Marissel links Watt's incoherent speech with decomposition of personality, with the theme of nothingness, and with the artist's imperatives which drive him beyond *"le degré zéro de l'écriture"*[14] to express the inexpressible. Mauriac correlates language with the hypothetical imperative: "Whoever speaks is carried along by the logic of language and its articulations. The hypothetical imperative is part of language and man's essence. Language imposes on us a system."[15]

However pertinent the work of these critics has been, it has left us with an incomplete, sometimes superficial view of the multiple structures of *Watt.* Until recently critical studies have emphasized thematics, and *Watt*'s themes have been analyzed primarily in terms of biographical factors—Beckett's mind—rather than in relation to other structural elements. With a few exceptions, this biographical-thematic orientation has been primarily the province of the French critics, who interest themselves in the relationship between Beckett's mental make-up and his choice of themes. Other critics have examined only particular aspects of structure, neglecting any correlations between theme and the other structural components of *Watt.*

Although the English-speaking critics seem to look at the work as a whole rather than as a random assortment of unrelated compositional elements, they frequently neglect nonetheless to describe and to emphasize the integration of structural components into the total design of *Watt.* They have often failed to recognize the intricately woven structural macrocosm that is *Watt,* a novel whose interrelated microcosmic structures have been undeservedly neglected.

The aim of this study is to try to give a comprehensive view of the integral unity of *Watt*'s structure. Instead of being content with examining the separate structural components of the novel, I shall go further in attempting to show their specific interrelationships in making up the total structure of the novel.

Among the critics of the theories of structure, I have drawn most valuabe insight for my own analysis from Eugene Falk, Edgar Roberts, Gérard Genette, Tzvetan Todorov and the Slavic formalist critics. Many critics previously cited, particularly Szanto, Federman, Cohn, and Hesla, have also proved invaluable for the understanding of *Watt*.

Before studying *Watt*'s structures, it would be wise at this point to quote Edgar Roberts' definition of structure and to explain how each of the novel's micro-structural components influences the macro-structure of the work:

> The word *structure* is in fact a metaphor, implying that a work of literature, both topically and emotionally, is as connected and unified as a building—a structure . . . . Structure is a matter of the relationships among parts that are usually described in terms of cause and effect, position in time, association, symmetry and balance and proportion . . . . The study of structure attempts to demonstrate that the idea and the resulting arrangement of parts produces a total impression.[16]

Jean Piaget elaborates on this idea. In his view:

> Structure is comprised of three key ideas: the idea of wholeness, the idea of transformation, and the idea of self-regulation . . . . Elements of a structure are subordinated to laws, and it is in terms of these laws that the structure *qua* whole or system is defined. Moreover, the laws governing a structure's composition are not reducible to cumulative one-by-one association of its elements: they confer on the whole as such over-all properties distinct from the properties of its elements.[17]

Thus the structure of literature should not be viewed atomistically as independent, static composites or "aggregates" but rather as self-contained yet interdependent substructures. "But in being treated as a substructure," Piaget goes on to say:

a structure does not lose its own boundaries; the larger structure does not 'annex' the substructure; if anything we have a confederation, so that the laws of the substructure are not altered but conserved and the intervening change is an enrichment rather than an impoverishment.[18]

And finally, in their work, *Literature: Form and Function,* Albert Duhamel and Richard Hughes understand a novel's structure to be essentially a matter of "form following function,"[19] as in architecture or engineering. Fundamentally, it is by virtue of its form, an objective, discoverable entity that is determined by its function, that any work of art possesses significance. The meaningfulness of Samuel Beckett's work lies in the genius of his creative ability to achieve a delicate balance of structure within seeming chaos. Taking as my point of departure the existence of the immanent integral entity of *Watt,* I will focus on the primary elements of syntactic, semantic, and verbal structures and the interrelationships existing between them, with the final object of viewing their synthesis in the total structure of the work.

Notes

[1]Alan Schneider, "Waiting for Beckett." in *Beckett at 60 : A Festschrift* (London: Calder and Boyars, 1967), p. 34.

[2]Samuel Beckett and Georges Duthuit, "Three Dialogues," in *Samuel Beckett: A Collection of Critical Essays,* ed. Martin Esslin (Englewood Cliffs, N. J. : Prentice-Hall, 1965), p. 21.

[3]Tom F. Driver, "Beckett by the Madeleine," *Columbia University Forum,* 4 (Summer 1961), p. 23.

[4]Beckett and Duthuit, p. 21.

[5]Raymond Federman, *Journey to Chaos: Samuel Beckett's Early Fiction* (Los Angeles: University of California Press, 1965), p. 132.

6*Narrative Consciousness* (Austin: University of Texas Press, 1972).

7*The Testament of Samuel Beckett* (New York: Hill and Wang, 1964).

8A. J. Leventhal, "The Beckett Hero," in *Samuel Beckett: A Collection of Critical Essays,* p. 46.

9William York Tindall, *Samuel Beckett* (New York: Columbia University Press, 1964), p. 19.

10Samuel Beckett, *Molloy* (New York: Grove Press, 1955), p. 13.

11Richard Coe, *Samuel Beckett* (New York: Grove Press, 1964). pp. 37-40.

12Hugh Kenner, *Samuel Beckett: A Critical Study* (New York: Grove Press, 1961), p. 99.

13*Langage et fiction dans le roman de Beckett* (Paris: Gallimard, 1969).

14André Marissel, *Samuel Beckett* (Pairs: Editions Universitaires, 1963), p. 25. Marissel borrows the phrase from Roland Barthes.

15Claude Mauriac, *The New Literature,* trans. Samuel I. Stone (New York: George Braziller, 1959), p. 81.

16Edgar V. Roberts, *Writing Themes about Literature* (Englewood Cliffs, N. J.: Prentice-Hall, 1969), p. 79.

17Jean Piaget, *Structuralism* (New York: Basic Books, 1970), pp. 5-7.

18*Ibid.,* p. 14.

19*Literature: Form and Function* (Englewood Cliffs, N. J.: Prentice-Hall, 1965), p. 454.

Chapter II

Character

Samuel Beckett composed *Watt* during World War II between 1942 and 1944 under very trying circumstances. He and his wife Suzanne had fled Paris with forged papers just ahead of the Gestapo which was rounding up a resistence group in which Beckett was involved. They eventually found refuge in Roussillon, a small town in the Vaucluse mountains of the Provence, where for the next two years they posed as ordinary French farmhands always in imminent danger of discovery. At night the author worked on his manuscript.[1]

Watt was the author's second novel, after *Murphy*,[2] and in view of Beckett's career is something of a landmark and anomaly. It was the last novel composed in English. Moreover, it also constitutes a departure in style and theme. *Murphy* is comic, lusty, although shot through with pathos, and it employs a realistic style. *Watt* is Beckett's first attempt to burst through the boundaries of the conventional novel. At first glance it is chaotic and formless yet, as we shall see, actually highly structured. It is a novel of failure and pathos, yet it is simultaneously comic. It is equipped with a minimal plot, deliberately confused, multi-leveled, multi-dimensional, subject to varying critical interpretations, enormously eloquent yet obscure, pedantic and intensely lyrical at the same time. Conventional literary criticism has not been able to come to terms with it. Hence the varying contradictory interpretations.

The novel is divided into four parts which are not necessarily developed in linear and logical sequence. In fact, the author has deliberately confused them. The basic plot is easily told. Watt, the central character journeys to the house of a certain Mr. Knott where he has found employment as a servant. He stays in Knott's employment for an indeterminate time, then leaves and makes another journey to an unknown destination. Sometime during that period— the exact time frame is not given—he is institutionalized.

It is interesting to note here that, thematically, the mental hospital forms the only major link with *Murphy*. The hero of the novel, Murphy, is employed as a nurse in such an institution. In *Watt* Beckett depicts the next dimension. Its hero becomes an inmate suffering from the clearly discernible effects of schizophrenia.[3]

Thus the link of institutionalized insanity between the two novels must also be viewed as an artistic progression on Beckett's part. In *Murphy* insanity forms a mere refuge in the background. In *Watt* it is a major focus of the setting.

a) *Character Structure*

Watt, as the hero of the novel, is surrounded by clusters of subsidiary characters as he engages himself on his mysterious journeys and labors. The only major exceptions, standing apart, are Knott and Arsene who will be discussed below. Watt—whose Christian name is never geven—appears in various physical manifestations which are fleeting and contradictory. There are five major physical descriptions of Watt experienced or described by several characters. The first occurs right at the beginning:

> Then it moved on, disclosing, on the pavement, motionless, a solitary figure, lit less and less by the receding lights, until it was scarcely to be distinguished from the dim wall behind it. Tetty was not sure whether it was a man or a woman. Mr. Hackett was not sure that it was not a parcel, a carpet for example, or a roll of tarpaulin, wrapped up in a dark paper tied about the middle with a cord.[4]

Thus Watt is introduced as a thing or a ghost rather than as a male homo sapiens. It might be observed that this descriptive passage has impressed a number of critics who tend to find it "typical" of

Watt. However, later on Goff Nixon, Tetty's husband, supplies an additional physical characteristic of Watt. He has a huge red nose.

A little later on, Watt is seen walking away from a train station complete with hat and bags. His extraordinary walk which bears some resemblance to the stance of the African Masai, arouses the attention of another secondary character, a Lady McCann, who thought it was a "funambulistic stagger."[5] Lady McCann eventually throws a stone at Watt which strikes his hat.

Watt's nose also catches the attention of Arsene, the servant in Knott's house, who introduces Watt into some of the mysteries of his new employment. Arsene sees some additional details of Watt's appearance: "But to return to Walter and Vincent, they were very much your height, breadth and width, that is to say big bony shabby seedy haggard knockkneed men with rotten teeth and big red noses . . . ."[6] Thus to Arsene Watt has the same appearance as Walter and Vincent. The fourth observation of Watt's physical appearance is made by Sam, a fellow inmate in the mental institution which appears in Part III, probably the most remarkable section of the novel. (Sam, who is suddenly revealed as the narrator or one of the narrators of the preceding parts, is not a character at all but, as we shall see in Chapter III, a very clever mechanism or device on Beckett's part to produce new dimensional levels of insanity and sanity through which his narration can be viewed alternately.) As seen by "Sam," Watt appears now in a state of rapid disintegration. He walks backward, collides with tree trunks, fences and underbrush, bloodies his face, and wears his clothes backwards. Most remarkable of all, his speech is gradually changing from a low non-stop murmur to complete inversion until he speaks words and sentences backward as well. It should be noted that this is the first time that Watt's voice and speech are described.[7] In the two preceding parts he was virtually silent.

In the final section of the novel Beckett gives a very elaborate and detailed description of Watt's appearance as he leaves Knott's establishment and goes on his final journey which ends the novel. This description is objective in the sense that it is not seen through the eyes of any character or attributed to a narrator.

Watt carries two bags and wears a hat which is of pepper color. We are even told of the origin of this hat. His grandfather had picked it up at the race track and its original color was mustard.

Watt also wears a greatcoat with nine buttons. It is greenish and there are patches of velvet on the collar. He is tie-less, without a collar, wears very baggy trousers (the rest of his attire is not enumerated because we are told it is not visible under the greatcoat) and his feet are shod in a boot and a shoe. Both are brownish in color and of different sizes. The boot is size twelve, the shoe ten and Watt's size is eleven. He is wearing both socks under the boot, none under the shoe.[8]

These five occasions for a description of Watt's appearance, manner of walking, voice and speech are, as noted before, fleeting and contradictory. In addition, they originate on various external levels. Thus, in Genette's phrase they can be said to be "externally focused." Actually, they are mere sub-structures of Watt's character which not only bear a balanced relationship to each other, but form an integrated entity. These sub-structures can be reduced as follows:

1) Watt —— a bundle with a red nose
2) Watt —— a figure walking like a contortionist (funambulist) or a figure violating the approved manner of the walking pattern of a good citizen; an extremist or deviant.
3) Watt —— a big, bony, shabby, haggard man with a red nose and bad teeth.
4) Watt —— a figure in reverse. Reverse walk, reverse speech and clothes worn in reverse. Disintegration.
5) Watt —— an odd character peculiarly dressed.

These elements are clearly related in a combination. If we add some further bits of notation strewn about the text to flesh them out, we obtain the following external structure of Watt as a character:

Watt, a big bony and gaunt man with a large red nose and sparse red hair goes about shabbily and peculiarly dressed. Apparently hails from Dublin, Ireland. Occupation unknown, possible intellectual *manqué*. Therefore takes menial employment as servant. Not unexpectedly in such cases of failure, suffers nervous breakdown. Spends some time in a mental institution.

Yet this is merely the structure of the character of Watt extrapolated from the text. The internal structure of Watt is more amorphous. It involves psychic activity, habits, mental activity such as reasoning and imagination, obsessions and other emotional states and, finally, time. Time in flux, time as a void, time in various dimensions, and time as a healer.

What are the characteristics of the internal Watt? Almost every commentator has described him as an indefatigable speculator, a spinner of hypotheses, a compulsive questioner, an obsessed seeker of solutions. This characterization has been eloquently summed up by Hugh Kenner: "He bears the Cartesian cross, the discursive intellect, with its irremediable itch to think explicable worlds into existence, stumbling through corridors of extreme absurdity toward some talismanic formula with which it can be temporarily at rest."[9]

On the surface this certainly rings true. Many pages are taken up by Watt's speculations on such matters as Knott's meal habits, the relationship of the remains of the meal to a hungry dog or dogs, the question of key and lock to the door of a fellow servant, the nature of Mr. Knott and similar matters. Ultimately, Watt, seeking a solution to every problem, fails and goes mad.

Yet this is too facile a definition. There is much more to Watt's internal character than compulsive spinning of hypotheses. Beckett has woven within the text fine strands of delicately balanced sub-structures which uncovered present a much more complex picture of Watt's character.

These strands can be listed as follows:

1) Watt is a kind, inoffensive man.
2) He does not complain when offended.
3) He is an intensely lyrical person.
4) His imagination often turns into music or poetry.
5) He enjoys daydreaming.

These major structures determine some other structures of his character which hover on the border between the internal and external.

Whatever their position their manifestation is vertically linked to purely internal structure in a logical progression:

6) Watt is a university graduate.

7) He probably specialized in philosophy, the study of logic, mathematics or mathematical probability.

8) He knows nothing of painting and physics.

9) He is constantly in need of money.

10) He suffers from several disorders. His skin breaks easily, his teeth are bad and he probably has some glandular or hormonal deficiency which prevents him from completing the sexual act.

11) He enjoys making love to women although these deficiencies result in semi-platonic rather than fully carnal relationships.

12) He drinks nothing but milk and his teeth are bad.

13) He is an experienced traveler.

Once again we can discern a clear link between these substructures forming a certain combination which presents an intensely human side of Watt. Thus with all these factors in mind, including Watt's negative qualities, we arrive at the following construction of Watt's personality structure:

Watt, a Dublin university graduate (Trinity College) who specialized in philosophy is an unemployable intellectual. He is an intellectual vagrant, an idler, given to intense bouts of speculation bearing on any and all human or non-material phenomena which can occupy him endlessly for the simple reason that he has plenty of time while at the same time having no conception of time. His intellect suffers from one crippling weakness, yet it also enjoys one asset. Watt cannot stop his discursive meditations until he has found a solution to whatever problem is under the microscope of his brain. This is a compulsion. At the same time, his intellect is so finely honed that he can arrive simultaneously at a number of solutions to the problem as well as a number of objections. In addition, he possesses the gift of discrimination and selection. However, he has no intuitive faculty. Unlike most men of his type, he can perform menial work when necessity calls for it. He has several physical weaknesses, is kind, inoffensive, non-aggressive. He feels deeply. Still, this combination is not a favorable one when confronted with the modern world. It is likely to lead to mental breakdowns.

Watt may be a hero, or rather anti-hero, or specifically, in Scholes' felicitous phrase, a hero who is "not an agent but a patient."10

It might be further observed Watt's character is a disturbingly familiar one. There are many Watts among us.

With this preparatory introduction to the main character, one can now proceed to a discussion of the structure of the character of Arsene, one of the two characters next in importance to Watt. Arsene makes his appearance when Watt arrives at Knott's establishment, delivers a "short" statement (it lasts twenty-four pages) and then takes his leave since he has been replaced by Watt.

The physical appearance of Arsene is the opposite of Watt. Arsene describes himself quite candidly as a "little fat shabby seedy juicy or oily bandylegged man, with a little fat bottom sticking out in front and a little fat belly sticking out behind."11

The inner Arsene also presents a contrast to Watt. He is a compulsive talker just as Watt is a compulsive thinker. His talk is an extraordinary mélange of the lyrical, of mysterious hints and of soaring descriptive passages of tremendous power. All this is infused with a sort of time mechanism as Arsene shifts elegantly from the past to the future and back so that his utterances have a sibylline quality.

What is this bald fat little man trying to convey by means of his several allusions to Watt's state? That Watt, having entered Knott's establishment has penetrated a world of constant flux, constant change, which nevertheless is timeless and motionless since its elements always return to the original state.12 In fact, there is no purpose behind this spectacle. Moreover, Knott who seems to be beyond the reach of this process, might be subject to its laws as well. Knott, too, must at some time have arrived and will leave sooner or later.

The perceptive Arsene knows that Watt's mind, forever in search of the perfect solution to any problem, cannot comprehend his philosophy. Watt's mind thinks in linear, rational, symmetrical terms where the element of time plays no role. Therefore, inevitably he will become time's victim.

Arsene's speech is the most important statement in the novel. Suffice it to say for the moment that it contains nothing less than Beckett's philosophy underlying *Watt* and other works. It will be examined in depth in Chapter IV.

After these considerations we can turn for comic relief to the secondary characters before tackling the problematic character of Knott. The subsidiary characters exist in three clusters which provide structural symmetry for the novel. There are, of course, other characters which appear in satirical talks or fantasies related throughout the novel, but they contribute nothing to the action and exist as mere illustrations.

The three groupings, then, are composed of a group of Irish citizens, obviously Dubliners (although the locale is never mentioned) who appear at the beginning and the end as a sort of chorus. In the center of the novel are Watt's mysterious fellow servants. Finally, we have Arsene and Knott.

The most important of these Dublin citizens who form a chorus at the beginning of the narration are Hackett, Mr. and Mrs. Goff Nixon, Spiro, Lady McCann, and at the end again Lady McCann, Nolan, Gorman, Cox, and Case. They live in a very simple world and Beckett wastes little description on them. They are essentially one-dimensional people who express themselves in one-dimensional dialogue which is the common-sense speech and sentiments of the average Dublin burgher:

> Night is falling fast, said Goff, soon it will be quite dark.
> Then we shall all go home, said Mr. Hackett.[13]

Or the following fragment in the end:

> When Watt saw a face on the other side of the window, he said:
> Give me a ticket, if you please.

He wants a ticket, cried Mr. Nolan.
A ticket to where? Said Mr. Gorman.
Where to? Said Mr. Nolan.
To the end of the line, said Watt.
He wants a ticket to the end of the line, cried Mr. Nolan.
Is it a white man? Said Lady McCann.[14]

This dialogue, which is marvelously realistic, deftly characterizes these people. Obviously Watt, by his appearance, his speech, and
his vague expressions violates all the norms of behavior which the
common Dubliners are used to. Fortunately Watt speaks English.
But, then, he might be an English-speaking foreigner. Perhaps a black
person? Who else would act so strangely?

There seems to be little question that Beckett deals harshly
with these philistines, including the half-mad Catholic editor Spiro
whom Watt meets on the train traveling to Knott's house. One is
tempted to express the opinions that Beckett settled some scores
here just as his master and friend James Joyce settled similarly some
scores in his work. These narrow-minded, bigoted Catholics described
by the Protestant Samuel Beckett were in part the reason James
Joyce fled to the Continent (just as perhaps Beckett fled his native
Dublin for Paris)—and they have helped make Watt what he is or
will be. This is the funny yet pathetic reality of Watt's world. Does
the road from this commonplace yet terrifying reality lead to an
insane asylum?

This thematic diversion indicates the structural function these
characters fulfill. The world of Dublin, as perceived by these bur-
ghers, begins the novel and ends the novel. In the middle lies a dimension of Dublin lying far beyond its everyday life, a dimension that
none of these good Dubliners will ever experience—unless they take
the same plunge that Watt does.

In the depths of the middle-narrative lies the other cluster of
secondary characters: Watt's fellow servants as well as Mrs. Gorman
and a man named Arthur who appears to have a mysterious connection
to Mr. Knott's establishment.

Of these characters, Erskine, Graves, Arthur, and Mrs. Gorman, only the last is fully realized beyond the status of serving a specific function in the plot as a mere mechanism or a symbol. This fish-woman, as Beckett calls her (of course, she sells fish), appears in only a short vignette of her love-making with Watt and she never speaks. What a masterfully drawn character in a magnificently comic yet pathetic vignette! Beckett has sketched in a few brief strokes so well the essence of this woman that we know virtually everything about her. She smells of fish; her left breast has been removed; she guzzles stout from the bottle; she conducts her affair with Watt with regular secrecy (only on Thursdays); and she is a complaisant old crone. She definitely does not make scenes—nor demands. Watt pleases her just as she pleases Watt. It is a comic yet decrepit Romeo and Juliet affair—without grandiose passions or tragedy. Or without youth.

Nor is it the middleaged passion of Anthony and Cleopatra. No titantic figures of grand eloquence. None of the heat of the Mediterranean or the exotic refinements and mysteries of Rome and Egypt. Merely shabby, hypocritical, rainy, lower class Dublin. So we see at once why Beckett was so successful with the character of Mrs. Gorman. Another score settled. Nonetheless he chose to give her a very minor part in the novel.

The character structure of Erskine is fairly simple. He has the same build as Arsene but unlike Arsene he never speaks to Watt except at the end when Watt has experienced speech difficulties. Aside from that occasion, "Erskine never opened his mouth, in Watt's presence except to eat, or belch, or cough, or keck, or muse, or sigh, or sing, or sneeze."[15] He is forever running up and down the stairs attending Mr. Knott, duties he performs ever so diligently.

Of his inner life we know virtually nothing except a brief remark by Arsene that Erskine is dreaming of promotion—which, of course, is a hopeless daydream.

Watt, burning with questions about the many mysterious circumstances of Knott's establishment, is too shy to ask the uncommunicative Erskine. This condition sets up the direction of the plot in the middle-narrative and discloses the essential function of Erskine: since Erskine does not talk, Watt gives over to speculation. His extended speculations culminate in his secret entry into Erskine's room and the discovery of a mysterious painting whose exceedingly important role as a symbolic support we shall discuss later.

Graves, the gardener, is a likable and talkative man with a queer manner of speech. He reveals a lot about Erskine, Arsene, and the previous servants but "nothing of interest." He also talks about Mr. Knott for whom his father and all his ancestors have worked and whose experiences were not apparently satisfactory. It is clear that Graves is a rambler of mere inconsequential tidbits who leaves Watt and the reader in the dark about the mysteries of the establishment. Yet Graves has a far more important problem on his mind about which he talks incessantly to Watt, as he had talked incessantly to Erskine and Arsene before that. Those two had given him advice which had failed; Watt cannot give him advice because the problem is beyond Watt's competence. In short, Mr. Graves' problem is his failing marriage, and that failure is clearly due to impotence.

Thus while we have a more successful two-dimensional character in Graves, it is also clear that the revelation of Graves' secret sorrow, this glimpse into his inner life, performs a strictly functional part in the structure of the book. It sets up the springboard for the much more important character of Arthur. This done, Graves' utility as a character has ended. His role is finished.

Arthur resembles Erskine and Arsene in appearance. He, too, is a fat little man. Moreover, he has a good deal in common with Arsene. He is intelligent, articulate, and just as compulsive a talker. During an encounter with Graves and Watt (Knott hovers in the background like a shadow), he advises Graves to try Bando, an aphrodisiac which can be taken in capsule form, and then launches into a hilarious, detailed account of a dissertation of a scholar named Louit and its presentation before a Grants Committee.

This speech lasts not less than twenty-seven pages and it discloses another characteristic of Arthur. His talent is clearly satiric. Like all good satire it is more of the brain than of the heart. Thus

Arthur is the opposite of Arsene who is of the heart, lyrical, poetic, philosophic, and sybilline.

Arthur was also a scholar like his homosexual friend Ernest Louit and his talk is peppered with informative details. However, it is quite obvious that he has never produced anything of scholarly distinction but is another failed intellectual—not like Watt, who compared to Arthur appears like a saintly figure, but a crafty type with more than a touch of the liar about him. He is not only an effective salesman for his product, Bando, but he also reveals detailed knowledge about customs procedures, regulations forbidding Bando, as well as ways of smuggling it. In short, Arthur is a criminal type of failed intellectual engaged in smuggling an aphrodisiac and selling it. Thus he is not only a modern figure, but a very contemporary figure: the man with a college education "pushing" drugs.

There is one element beyond all this which discloses to us the true character of Arthur, the "very nice open fellow," as he appears to Watt. This spellbinding snake oil salesman and intellectual swindler has a secret compulsion: he periodically returns to Knott's establishment because he cannot absent himself long from its mysteries or their permanence and stability, their "fixity."

Nevertheless, this latter element as well as the other aspects of Arthur's character cannot rescue it from its purely utilitarian stagecraft function. The occurrence of Arthur's periodic return is part of the structure of the action which we shall discuss in detail in the next chapter. As for Arthur's other functions, it is quite clear that he serves as a convenient tool of satire to take care of Graves' problem as well as to deliver a body blow at academic obscurantism and pedantry. It might be noted in passing that Samuel Beckett, M. A., who had served as a lecturer at Trinity College, was not unacquainted with the foibles of academic life.

If this group of characters, with the exception of Mrs. Gorman, is drawn more for functional purposes than for intrinsic interest and, consequently inner depth, then the polymorphic Mr. Knott operates on an entirely different scale. He gazes on the proceedings of the novel like the sun or the moon (which at first arouse Watt's dislike), but while he may be majestically distant in one sense he is very much within our reach, or rather Watt's reach, in another. For instance, during the final stage of his service, Watt helps him get ready for bed. Knott dons his night-shirt over his dayclothes and rises in the morning with his dayclothes over his nightshirt.

Now it must be remembered that all the information conveyed about Knott, (very baffling information it is) is diffused through the distorting lenses of various characters. There is, first of all, Watt who tells Sam of the details of his service to Knott. Sam is quite cognizant of the fact that Watt's reminiscences of Knott are incomplete, may be biased and distorted. For, in order to round out the picture of Knott, the narrator lacks the testimony of the other servants, Arsene, Erskine, Walter, and Vincent, for instance. "Then we would have had Erskine's Mr. Knott, and Arsene's Mr. Knott, and Walter's Mr. Knott, and Vincent's Mr. Knott, to compare with Watt's Mr. Knott. That would have been a very interesting exercise. But they all vanished, long before my time."16

This narrator is probably Sam. (He is not named.) If it is indeed Sam then it must be noted that the portrait of Knott is related by Watt to Sam, his fellow inmate in a mental institution. Obviously, Sam is not an entirely reliable witness whose testimony would be given credence in a court of law or by a historian. One the other hand, the information about Knott which Watt conveys was absorbed by him in the final stage of his service when his mind and speech had already begun to deteriorate. Thus, the portrait has passed through the reminiscent faculties of two madmen. Finally, if the mysterious narrator, quoted above, who speaks of "Watt's Mr. Knott," is not Sam but still another personality, then the information has been distorted by still another viewpoint. In short, whatever we know about Knott goes through a complex sifting process in various minds, yet is severely structured.

The structure of the narrative portrait that emerges of Knott can be reconstructed in this way: Knott via Watt via Sam or Knott via Watt via unknown narrator via Sam. Another variant of this structure would be Knott via unknown narrator via Watt via Sam.

This structure functions horizontally or vertically. The result is the same.

What is the result?

The result is that Knott appears as figure of figuration—the term "character" must be used with utmost caution in this context —which is not only larger than life but appears as a force, a cosmic force, which dominates Watt and the novel. Yet this figure, at the beginning when Watt is not in direct contact with him, still has some recognizable although odd human features. By the time Watt has been "promoted" to serve him, Knott has already expanded and keeps on expanding until he appears as a universal force or principle that transcends every known physical law. Interestingly enough, it is precisely at this point, when Watt is in direct contact with this apparition, that Watt's powers of speculation no longer come into play.

Knott, through Watt and Sam, is elaborately described. Here is the beginning portion of the description of his physical appearance:

> With regard to the so important matter of Mr Knott's physical appearance, Watt had unfortunately little or nothing to say. For one day Mr Knott would be tall, fat, pale and dark, and the next thin, small, flushed and fair, and the next sturdy, middlesized, yellow and ginger, and the next small, fat, pale and the next middlesized, flushed, thin and ginger, and the next tall, yellow, dark and sturdy, and the next . . . . [17]

The description continues in this vein for nearly two pages.

However, Watt cannot remember what Knott's face looked like. No wonder. Watt by now is so completely under the spell of his mysterious master who appears to him as an elemental force that his prodigious powers of reasoning and observation have collapsed. Knott, therefore, can do or be anything. He can change his appearance, his shape, his habits, his ways of eating and singing (or belching); he can disappear at will and reappear. He seems to be composed of different dimensions, different and opposing elements, atoms which ceaselessly circle. Yet all these contradictions, chaotic and confusing, nevertheless form a perfect balance of harmony.

Of course, there are times when some human quality shines through this cosmic picture. Knott sings in a monotonous tone, using words which have no meaning to Watt. (At this point it is disclosed that Watt was "a very fair linguist.") At other times he shouts obscure words in incomprehensible sequences such as "Excelmans! Cavendish! Habbakuk! Ecchymose!" His sheets are changed regularly on St. Patrick's Day. In addition, we know already from the scraps of information and observations that Watt had picked up in the beginning when he was not in direct contact with Knott that Knott had a mysterious arrangement for his meals, that he had not visitors, received no phone calls and little mail, stayed mostly in his room upstairs except to walk in the garden. He never left the grounds.

But these scraps of knowledge become completely obliterated under the impact of this chaotic, polymorphic figure that Knott represents when Watt is at the end in direct contact with him. Watt is completely overwhelmed. And so, at the end, he knows nothing concrete of Knott: "Of the nature of Mr Knott himself Watt remained in particular ignorance."[18]

It goes without saying that Knott, as a "character" or rather as a major phenomenon in the novel, also presents a major puzzle. So far the outward verbal structure of Knott, its somewhat arbitrary and confusing nature, has been presented. The conventional temptation is to plunge ahead, as previous critics have attempted, to "interpret" Knott without further ado. However, this temptation must be resisted. Knott, like all the characters, certainly the major ones, cannot be so quickly and glibly defined because he is composed of a variety of additional structural levels which must be carefully uncovered and analyzed.

b) *The Characters as Linguistic Experiments*

As manifested already in *Murphy* and even in shorter pieces, such as his earlier poems, stories and articles, Beckett had shown himself to have committed himself firmly to a non-realistic, experimental style in the English language. Heavily spiced with puns, anagrams, aphorisms, literary, poetical, philosophical, and historical allusions which he drew from his vast reading, Beckett's writing plunged ahead, disregarding the fashions of the day which called more and more for a simplified, journalistic language in the novel. Already, in 1929, at the age of twenty-three, Beckett made his future intentions very clear. He contributed a critical essay in defense of Joyce's work in progress to a volume of essays by friends of Joyce called *Our Exagmination Round His Factification for Incamination of Work in Progress,*19 which strongly supported Joyce's linguistic experiments.

> This inner elemental vitality and corruption of expression imparts a furious restlessness to the form, which is admirably suited to the purgatorial aspect of the work. There is an endless verbal germination, maturation, putrefaction, the cyclic dynamism of the intermediate. This reduction of various expressive media to their primitive economic directness, and the fusion of these primal essences into an assimilated medium for the exteriorisation of thought is pure Vico, and Vico, applied to the problem of style.20

Many critics slighted this important essay, possibly because they could not cope with the complex problem of the influence of Vico's philosophy of history on Beckett. We shall have occasion to refer to this seminal work repeatedly.

At any rate, the overwhelming and immediate impact on the young Beckett was the master of linguistic experimentation, James Joyce. In 1931 Beckett collaborated on the translation of the *Anna Livia Plurabelle*21 selection of the "work in progress" into French. This was an amazing piece of daring for a person to whom French was not a native language, especially given the complexities of Joyce's English. The translation was actually completed by Beckett's friend, Alfred Peron, whose eventual arrest by the Gestapo in Paris in 1942 was to lead to Beckett's flight to the Vaucluse where he composed *Watt.* By then Joyce had died, but the "work in progress" had, of course, become *Finnegans Wake.*

On the structural level of character in *Watt,* Beckett has performed a number of interesting linguistic experiments and permutations which not only invest the characters with additional dimensions but overlay them with thematic aspects.

There are, first of all, the characters' names. These have caused some amusing and unconvincing "interpretations" on the part of some critics.[22] It is obvious that one needs to delve deeply and not to be misled by some of Beckett's playful puns. A thorough, scientific examination of character structure will help to prevent us from being diverted by mere playfulness on the part of the author.

If one examines the names of the principal and secondary characters, one immediately discerns an interesting structural arrangement. There are two groupings, those with Irish surnames and those with names of non-Irish origin. In the latter category are Knott, Watt, Arsene, Graves and Spiro. It need not be stressed that the second group includes the most important characters.

One can easily dispose of the names of the minor characters in this group, Spiro and Graves. Spiro's name is clearly Greek in origin. (One need merely refer to the first name of a recent Vice President of the United States.) It gives us a Mediterranean flavor. It is also indubitably Jewish, most likely of that branch of Jewry known as Sephardic whose people were numerous in Greek-speaking areas.[23]

Spiro is given another nominal characteristic also: he explains candidly to Watt that his friends name him "Dum" because he is so bright and cheerful. Not only is Dum the anagram of "mud," but "dum" suggests stupidity in English and German. This quality Spiro confirms at once. Yet he is the editor of "Crux," a "popular catholic monthly," and a mad neo-Thomist popularizer. In naming Spiro, Beckett's linguistic play builds various structural characteristics from which flows an effective satire. The consolidation of these characteristics yields this portrait:

> Spiro, a Dubliner, popular Catholic editor. Actually of alien, non-Irish origin, possibly a convert. A stupid, bumbling man, enthralled by the extreme and obscure aspects of a religion which is still new to him. Thanks to his name and background his road to clerical office is barred, therefore he is only employable through pseudo-religious popularizing magazine. Like all converts he is an inveterate crusader for his new cause or religion.

Graves, the gardener in Knott's house, has an English or Anglo-Saxon name. "Graves," "grave," or "groves" originally meant a "small wood." The term is admirably suited to Graves' work since Knott's garden contains many trees and bushes. Moreover, Graves' funny way of pronouncing his "th's" pleases Watt, for in Graves' pronunciation "third" and "fourth" emerge as "turd" and "fart," "venerable saxon words" which Watt enjoyed. All of Graves' paternal ancestors worked in Knott's garden which was created by them, as noted before. Gardening is, of course, an English specialty and gardens have lent themselves to much mythologizing. Finally, "grave" in its present meaning is related to the original meaning of "graves"— it evolved from it inasmuch as graveyards began to be located in small, wooded garden plots. The character Graves, of course, is not only digging in Knott's garden, he is digging his marriage's grave with his impotence.

Once again we can construct as follows:

> Graves, a gardener, originally of English origin which he betrays by certain ways of pronouncing the "th." Occupation, typically English by ancestry. Tea-drinker, discreet, impotent, marriage problem. Anglo-Irish.

But the names of these two characters are merely linguistic play-things for Beckett in his novel. We now turn to the principal characters' names. First, Watt.

Watt's name is clearly of English origin. Apparently it originated in the name Walter which even after the Norman Conquest was still pronounced without the "l" sound. From this name was derived Wat which became Watt, Watts, Waters, Watson, Watkins, and other similar forms. All of these names designate people who "lived by the water."[24] We can now appreciate why Arsene upon first meeting Watt makes a joke about Wat Tyler (the peasant rebel) and later plays on Watt's name as "eyewater."

There are interesting variations that can be rung on Beckett's choice of the name Watt. Why is Watt so attracted to Mrs. Gorman the fishwoman? Obviously, fish and water go together. Moreover, keeping in mind the expert treatment of astrological lore displayed by Beckett in *Murphy*, we uncover another structure: Pisces and Aquarius have a great affinity for each other. And Watt by his psychological and intellectual makeup falls clearly under the zodiac sign of Aquarius. It should be noted that some types of Aquarians are considered to be more spiritual than sensual lovers. They are also impractical people. At any rate, both signs deal with water.

There are antitheses as well. The most famous namesake of Watt, one James Watt, invented the steam engine. Watt is, of course, also used as a measure of electrical power. Both symbolize concepts opposed to the plodding, impractical, speculatory Watt. Finally, Watt, according to Goff Nixon, for some reason did not like water.

Another category of structures lies in the mere word puns which can be played on Watt's name. However, since they are linked with Knott's name, they will be discussed along with Knott's name. For the moment, these are the additional structures of nomenclature we can add to our growing characterization of Watt:

> Watt, of English descent, Anglo-Irish. Zodiac sign: Aquarius. Water-bearer. Therefore attracted to Pisces. Apparently sun and moon not prominent in horoscope. According to birth period impractical and very unconventional. Given to much speculation.

Who is Knott or rather what is Knott?

The name is not only of English origin but, in turn, can be derived etymologically from the Danish. It must be noted that before 1066 A. D., Danes exerted much influence in England and crossbred considerably with the Angles as well as the Saxons. A number of words in current English can be thus traced to that period. In this case, the Danish Knut or Cnut became Englished as Knott. The original means "knot" in Danish.[25]

With this fact, we have uncovered a structural main artery, a connotative seme in Roland Barthes' definition, which points an index finger at the significance of the Watt-Knott relationship.[26] For it is quite clear that Watt not only has a master-servant relationship with Knott but that he is trying in vain to discover answers about that mysterious figure Knut/Knot/Knott. This knot/Knott proves insoluble.

Having established this structural function of Knott's name, one can illustrate the multi-faceted possibilities of its relation to Watt which have been touched upon before:

Watt/Knott	What is Knott?
Watt/Knot	What is knot?
Watt/not	Watt is knot
What/Knott	Watt is not
	What is not
What/knot	Watt is Knott
What/knot	What-not

or amplified in an excerpt from the so-called "addenda" of the novel:

Watt will not
abate one jot
but of what . . . .

that is of what
Watt will not
abate one tot.[27]

Clearly, the name Knott functions as a main structural seme by itself.

The last character's name to be analyzed is Arsene. The name is a proper name in French. One scholar has seriously suggested that Beckett derived this name from Balzac's *Louis Lambert*. This was hardly necessary. When Beckett wrote *Watt* he not only knew

French, but he was also living in France where Arsene is an uncommon though plausible name. Yet what Irishman bears such a name? There is the teaser of an antithesis here.

Or is Arsene symbolically not Irish at all? His speech to Watt discloses some interesting details. He is short, fat, and bald. He is educated. Arsene's concave chest reminds his tutor of the Battle of Crécy in the Hundred Years' War. It should be noted that in this battle, the massed English infantry massacred the French knights, so that the concave chest could mean symbolically defeat through wounding or death. Arsene is, as noted before, extremely articulate, penetrating yet lyrical. His utterances are also philosophical and prophetic. At the same time, they are concrete as well. Thus in a brilliant passage describing a servant girl's eating and digestive processes with striking realism, or rather naturalism, Arsene reminds one of Emile Zola's description of Paris as *"le ventre."* Arsene is obviously a fastidious servant from a cosmopolitan background. He has spent some time in London. Finally, he makes the revealing statement ". . . that then it was living and now it is dead, which is what you might call what I think the English call six of one and a half a dozen of the other, do they not, might you not? Or do I confuse them with the Irish?"[28]

This excerpt has a sudden, unmistakably foreign flavor and is made from the viewpoint of an outsider. It is impossible to believe that an Englishman or an Irishman could make such a statement. These linguistic threads suggest that Arsene functions symbolically on a level other than the one described earlier. His cultural codes are evident. He is French as well as whatever else he is. Watt, before Arsene leaves, sees him as two men.

Thus the various linguistic puns, allusions, and permutations of language result in these additional composite structures of Arsene:

> Arsene: Typical Frenchman in appearance. Educated, cosmopolitan, fastidious dresser. Possibly homosexual. Very articulate, voluble, excitable, penetrating, philosophical. Doppelganger.

The conceptual implications of these "un-Irish" names and their symbolic interpretations will be analyzed later. In the meantime we might consider some additional characteristics of their speech patterns.

Arsene's speech, as we have mentioned, consists of a voluble English with touches of foreign flavors. Graves betrays through his pronunciation of the "th" a degree of regression. He relapses into "venerable saxon words." Spiro exhibits a compulsion to refer to foreign obscure saints and foreign localities. Knott says virtually nothing at all, with two exceptions: he sings words whose meaning to the "very fair linguist" Watt is incomprehensible or he "ejaculates" a quatrain of sphinx-like, semi-obscure expressions. Watt, on the other hand, offers the most elaborate linguistic case study of them all.

He is either silent or speaks in fairly clear, polite, short sentences. Yet, at certain intervals he is subject to dreams in which he composes musical verse. These poetic creations are obscure, but it should be noted for the moment that the number four fulfills an important symbolic function in them just as it does in the four main sections of the novel.

But the *chef d'œuvre* of Watt's linguistic utterances is, of course, their eventual decline into what could be termed anti-language. This process is elaborately described in the section dealing with the mental institution; yet, one must recall again that the account of Watt's lapse into what appears at first glance to be gibberish is related by his fellow inmate, Sam, an unreliable informer. The main characteristic of this anti-language or gibberish lies in the inversion of words or sentences. One critic, Ruby Cohn, has painstakingly listed the entire process of this decline.[29] Yet the words and sentences betray Watt's indestructible rationality. It is fairly easy to reconstruct them into English. For example, in this "advanced" case of his deterioration: "Deed did taw tonk. Tog da wat? Tonk. Luf puk saw? Hap! Deen did Tub? Ton sparp. Tog da tub? Ton wonk."[30] It will be noted that the words "tonk" and "ton," inversions of "knot" and "not," appear rather frequently in this short excerpt. Watt simply could not get Knott off his mind.

Beckett's carefully devised linguistic experiments reflecting Watt's decline of language might have a far more mundane background, not altogether dependent upon Beckett's artistic imagination and skill. G. C. Barnard has shown that they represent very good examples of schizophrenic speech disorders.31 In other words, they do occur among deviant personalities in real life.

Beckett's preoccupation with mental institutions had already started in *Murphy*. On the other hand, he was no stranger to examples of severe mental illness around him. Joyce's daughter Lucia, who conceived a violent but unrequited passion for Beckett, had to be institutionalized repeatedly. Not even the skill of Carl Gustav Jung could cure her mental disorders.

Summing up, we can postulate that the various speech patterns employed by these characters significantly add to their artistic structure.

c) *Relationship—Antithesis, Synthesis, Transformation*

In the preceding analysis of the character structures, a number of references have been made to the position of the characters vis-à-vis each other and vis-à-vis the direct linkage of these stances on plot and theme. For example, to state the most obvious fact, the central character Watt entertains a certain relationship with Knott which in turn results in certain actions or behavior on the part of Watt. This cause and effect principle, in turn, illustrates a significant thematic aspect of the narrative.

To be sure, such a scheme is a simplistic representation. There are other complex elements involved. Some of these elements by their very complexity and the prominence given to them in the novel can overwhelm the analyst. Others, just as important though understated, can be underestimated. The all-important principle of a harmonious and integral relationship between the various structures can be lost among the details. Nevertheless, the above scheme contains in kernel the essence of our hypothesis.

It is immediately obvious that Watt, at the center of the novel's stage, occupies an antithetical relationship with various characters, aside from Knott, indeed with groups of characters. This structural adversary arrangement is determined simultaneously by

Watt's character and actions or non-actions and by the same deter-
minants on the part of the other characters which thus operate upon
each other. Here is a linear, schematic representation of Watt's adversary relationships in the narrative:

> Watt versus Dubliners (Hackett, Nixon, Spiro, McCann)
> Watt versus Arsene
> Watt versus Erskine
> Watt versus Graves
> Watt versus unknown narrator
> Watt versus Arthur
> Watt versus Knott
> Watt versus Mrs. Gorman
> Watt versus Sam
> Watt versus himself (Watt)
> Watt versus Knott (again)
> Watt versus Dubliners

or to reduce this to groupings of characters:

> Watt versus Dubliners
> Watt versus Knott
> Watt versus fellow servants
> Watt versus Sam
> Watt versus Knott
> Watt versus Dubliners

One aspect becomes immediately evident from these schemas—that
of the grand structure of the novel. It is a harmonious, circular entity.

On the other hand, at first glance, some objections could be
raised to some of these opposing stances. Has it not been demonstrated that, rather than an adversary relationship, there existed a
strong affinity between Watt and Mrs. Gorman?

Indeed it has, to judge by the symbolic and thematic levels we
have seen embedded in the text. Yet, concurrent with these levels
one catches a glimpse of a paradoxical opposition. Beckett freely
discusses the dialectic tension of affinity-opposition in a long, philosophical passage which analyzes the opposing elements of the characters of Watt and Mrs. Gorman before concluding with no conclusion:

"All is possible." What is possible? That all opposing elements can simultaneously attract and repulse each other. In a concluding after-thought, Watt himself reflects on this hypothesis in concrete terms: Mrs. Gorman was attracted to him by the bottle of stout, he to her by her smell of fish. In other words, a fusion of opposites.

This passage illustrates the action which occurs. On still another level it illustrates a major thematic aspect of the novel which, by the way, is, in turn, evidenced by the linguistic maneuvers Beckett employs in his analysis of the relationship. He brilliantly balances opposing elements. Form becomes content.

The analysis of the above example results in a key deduction: the antithesis between the characters is resolved by synthesis. The opposing structures of sub-structures meet and fuse, simultaneously or in stages. The order or sequence of such events does not matter. For the time element which would normally govern this sequence or non-sequence has been abolished. Or rather it has assumed a dif-ferent form and quantity as well as quality. This idea, too, has im-portant, thematic reverberations which we shall discuss in a later chapter. But the reader will already recognize a variant of the Ein-steinian theory of things existing and taking on meaning relative to their position vis-à-vis other things.

Thus Watt becomes Knott[32] just as Sam becomes Watt or Lady McCann becomes Mrs. Gorman, *ad infinitum.* One can play this game indefinitely in any direction. Yet the game always describes a circle. In a subsequent chapter, I will demonstrate that this circle is finally the ultimate structural and philosophical figure of *Watt.*

We have spoken of antithesis and synthesis in Beckett's char-acters. There is a third principle or structural law involved here which sometimes runs parallel, sometimes diverges, but is always linked with the elements of antithesis and synthesis until it reaches the plateau of the circle. This is transformation.

The relationship between the characters acquires through synthesis the additional element of bi-polarity. Although opposed, they have sought each other, completed or complemented each other, in fact, identified with each other. Watt suddenly discovers he is the same height as Knott. Both wear shoes on only one foot. Sam has a strong physical affinity for Watt and walks with him, hands placed on shoulders in a complicated physical movement like one human being or rather like Siamese twins joined together. Or, philosophically, to quote Arsene in his prophetic utterances, there is a reversed metamorphosis. Laurel turns into Daphne, Theseus kisses Ariadne, Ariadne Theseus. Arthur who can only tell his stories "far" from Knott, yet returns to Knott's house to write entries in his journal. And finally

> Watt will not
> abate one jot
> but of what
>
> of the coming to
> of the being at
> on the going from
> Knott's habitat
>
> of the long way
> of the short stay
> of the going back home
> the way he had come . . . .[33]

Thus Watt who has entered Knott's "habitat," hoping to solve its mysteries, its "what," has ironically been transformed by them into a madman. He, nevertheless, returns to Knott. To do what? To start the serial cycle again by trying to solve the mystery of Knott who functions "in a vermicular series," in short, in a cycle. And, of course, Watt will fail again *ad infinitum.*

Transformation, therefore, means that characters who have completed each other through synthesis have merged their elements in bi-polarity, have acquired a new mingled identity which is in a way a new character begotten by them or emerging from their union. But this union and the fruit of their union, the transformed phenomena, last for only a few brief moments because their ultimate essence is illusion. They separate, just as Arsene finally appears as a double image, go their divergent ways only to resume the cycle again, to merge in synthesis and so on. The cycle appears to be self-regulatory and works ever towards a harmonious whole. All is balanced, all is inter-related, irrespective of opposing tendencies and changes through transformation; yet each stage is illusion. Knott is Watt and what is not.

d) *Conceptual Implications*

What do all of these notions mean in terms of Beckett's characters or, to put it more precisely, what implications can we deduce from the above analyses as far as the characters of *Watt* are concerned?

Beckett, long before he wrote *Watt,* made an interesting statement: "The danger is the neatness of identification."[34] As usual, he did not explain, a habit he was to adopt permanently. He was referring specifically to Proustian characters, yet, regardless of the circumstances, it is obvious to the reader of Beckett that the thrust of these words became embedded in the programme of his future work. He is and remains the most puzzling artist in contemporary Western literature.

Our analysis of the characters in *Watt* has hopefully laid bare their intrinsic structures. Yet, as has been demonstrated above, these structures, while producing a harmonious character entity which can function independently, simultaneously produce ambiguous character-entities entertaining ambivalent relationships with other ambiguous character-entities. In other words, the characters are not only multifaceted and multilayered but their symbolic projections operate the same way. Yet they are not solitary chameleons. Their changes occur not only on the inside but in exterior relationships as well. These changes are ceaseless.

Thus when we ask what is the "meaning" of X in *Watt* we are not only using an imprecise term, in the Beckettian sense, we are also using an exhausted linguistic term.

Still, our tool is linguistic and our intent critical; and we must cope with Beckett's subject (in this case, the characters), as best we can, within what Beckett imagines are its intellectual and linguistic limitations. For we must never forget that *Watt* is Beckett's view, just as Knott is Watt's Knott and not Arsene's or Erskine's Knott— all filtered through Sam, the madman. Yet having stated this, the door has suddenly opened. We are not superimposing our imprecise, imperfect rational conceptions à la Watt who only finds closed doors without keys; we are adopting, as best we can, the magical tool that Watt lacks. We shall try to see the characters through Sam, that is, Sam Beckett's eyes.

In this dimension there are no certainties, only possibilities. In fact, "all is possible." This permits us at once to tackle the shadow that is the character of Sam, the narrator, who divides himself like a cell to provide other nameless narrators in the récit. We have called him before a "mere device," a mechanism. That is his function, a function which he fulfills admirably by giving us a pretty coherent account of the adventures of a madman named Watt. This is no mean feat, as Sam states on numerous occasions. For even considering the numerous distortions and omissions to which must be added the incoherences of Watt's language, Sam brings it off. Sam, the chronicler of a madman's adventures, is also a fellow inmate in a madhouse. Which produces the delicious possibility that Sam may be sane and mad at the same time, a condition not unknown to mankind and one that Beckett uses, as noted before, for thematic and plot effects. These possibilities will be explored in other sections of this study. Suffice it to say for our purposes that Sam apparently is perfectly sane and objective when considering Watt's condition, that is, the outside world, and mad when considering his own affairs in his own world. He likes to play horrible games with rats and larks' nests.

Seen from this vantage point the character structure of Watt is lit up by the possibilities of a new conception. Watt, an Anglo-Irish intellectual manqué of middle age, arrives at the establishment of Mr. Knott, an establishment whose mysteries force him into endless speculations (and inventions) which eventually are fruitless and drive him mad. Strangely enough, before arriving at Knott's he does not speculate. After leaving Knott he does not speculate either. Not that he lacks opportunity. A superb occasion presents itself for endless theological and philosophical *contretemps* with Spiro. For instance, they might have argued about the mystery of the immaculate conception or even given a thousand reasons pro and con regarding the existence of God. Watt would have excelled in the latter department, yet he does nothing. He does not even pay close attention. A Joycean character might have plunged in. Why does Watt's mind not react? It is not stimulated by the religious atmosphere of Catholic Dublin. Watt, in short, might be a Protestant, a situation not unlikely given his ancestry.

Yet, as soon as he arrives at Knott's house his speculations begin. He seeks the talismanic formula that will exorcise his constant seeking. What was that magic formula which caused his ceaseless seeking which he could not stop? The cause and effect of simple things, of material things, of things immediately glanced, of apparent phenomena. "But whatever it was that Watt saw, with the first look, that was enough for Watt, that had always been enough for Watt, more than enough for Watt."35

And so Watt seeks for entrances, for dogs, for pots, for locks, for keys, for bells, for telephones or buzzers and so on. But even here he does not inquire. For he presupposes that the condition or thing he has glimpsed yet which immediately does not reveal all requires a solution, a formula. But supposing that no forumla was required because the situation or the thing did not need it?

That state was impossible for Watt to grasp because it did not exist in his universe. Watt lacked magic. What did that magic consist of? Intuition and a sense of the comic, of the comic of *La Comédie Humaine,* of the comic of *La Comédie de l'Univers.*

Watt never laughed. Not even after a "little voice" told him hilarious incidents which supposedly accounted for Knott's habit of leaving his meal or part of his meal to a dog. Another character, say Arsene, might have laughed the whole thing off and let it go at that. Watt sought the absent dog and, finding none, spun a fantastic tale which would finally account for Knott's arrangement—which may not have existed in the first place.

The absence of intuition, the gift to grasp in a flash the essence hidden by the deceiving skin of the obvious, left Watt only with his scholastic intellect which tended solely towards the logical, symmetrical formula. Skepticism was unknown to him. Poetry and music occurred to him only when he could sporadically but never successfully free himself from the inexorable demands of his thinking machine. Yet the mechanism of the thinking machine would, on the way to the magic formula, produce clouds of solutions and objections which formed nebulae, gaseous fantasies which eventually engulfed him. Had he only possessed the magic of the comic, even its lower form, mere humor, he would have been able to dissolve those speculative clouds of fantasy. He might have been able to grasp the ultimate truth which Arsene tried to convey to him, knowing all the time that Watt would never grasp it. Instead Watt possessed the mere pathetic or pathos (*das fruchtbare bathos der Erfahrung,* as Beckett says in the "addenda").

We must, of course, produce Arsene as a commentator before stating our final conceptual conclusions. Mr. or M. Arsene, the seer. Arsene of concave chest with breast feathers—the complementary symbol for Tiresias' mammalia? Arsene, who should be a Cartesian but who turns out to be a Bergsonian—who tells or tries to tell Watt of many things, of the illusions of time, of the unending change, of laughter and its supreme form, "the laugh that laughs—silence please—at that which is unhappy."[36] Yet Watt never interrupts nor does he understand.

Arsene makes one of his final thrusts in this vein with the following excerpt:

> Or is there a coming that is not a coming to a going that is not a going from, a shadow that is not the shadow of purpose, or not? For what is this shadow of the going in which we come, this shadow of the coming in which we go, this shadow of the coming and the going in which we wait, that budding withers, that withering buds, whose blooming is a budding withering? I speak well, do I not, for a man in my situation.[37]

A brilliant segment which closes brilliantly with the comic. The deadly serious leavened by the comic that takes the cosmic condition of ceaseless flow, and with it the human condition, not seriously at all. Why? Because in the end it does not matter. Even the illusion of reality does not matter.

To return to Watt, the pursuer of meaning which leaves him indifferent since meaning itself requires still further pursuit to uncover the ultimate solution—which does not exist. He therefore has to invent meanings as well as problems which apparently require meanings and therefore further pursuit after the solution. The inventions are the gaseous fantasies noted before, the "fancies" Watt was subject to, especially during his final stay in Knott's house, as unknown narrator alias Sam informs us in the beginning of the second section of the novel, which grew along with Watt's decline. Or grew because of Watt's decline.

Resuming our own structural strands, if Watt was a ceaseless pursuer of problems and solutions to the obvious or of trifles or if he invented problems where none existed to pursue solutions then it is possible, not inevitable but possible, that he might have served in an establishment, Knott's establishment, which was perfectly ordinary. As was his master, Mr. Knott. Or, give and take a bit, perhaps slightly odd. If, on the other hand, in this "tale told by an idiot," to quote Shakespeare, Watt pursued meanings which were not, mysteries which were not—solutions to problems which were not—just as Knott was not—then what is Knott becomes once again for naught. What or what/not, the ultimate solution which is no solution. It does not exist because Knott and his establishment did not exist, except in Watt's head. Only Dublin and its people are real, but they produce the illusion which Watt pursues towards a solution in a house somewhere in its outskirts, near the race course. Is that house, Knott's establishment, the same as the mental institution?

Arsene exits laughing.

Notes

[1]Hugh Kenner, *A Reader's Guide to Samuel Beckett* (New York: Farrar, Straus and Giroux, 1973), p. 73. Hugh Kenner, *Samuel Beckett, A Critical Study* (New York: Grove Press, 1961), pp. 22-24. Kenner is one of the handful of critics who have bothered to mention the extraordinary conditions under which *Watt* was composed.

[2]Samuel Beckett, *Murphy* (New York: Grove Press, 1957).

[3]G. C. Barnard, *Samuel Beckett: A New Approach* (New York: Dodd, Mead & Company, Inc., 1970), p. 24.

[4]Samuel Beckett, *Watt* (New York: Grove Press, 1959), p. 16.

[5]*Ibid.*, p. 31.

[6]*Ibid.*, p. 58.

[7]*Ibid.*, p. 156.

[8]*Ibid.*, p. 219.

[9]Kenner, *Samuel Beckett,* pp. 59-60.

[10]Robert Scholes, *Structuralism in Literature* (New Haven: Yale University Press, 1974), p. 110.

[11]*Watt*, p. 58.

[12]*Ibid.*, pp. 41-45.

[13]*Ibid.*, p. 16.

[14]*Ibid.*, p. 244.

[15]*Ibid.*, p. 85.

[16]*Ibid.*, p. 126.

[17]*Ibid.,* p. 209.

[18]*Ibid.,* p. 199.

[19]Paris, 1929.

[20]*Ibid.,* p. 16.

[21]Samuel Beckett, "Anna Livia Plurabelle," *Nouvelle Revue Française* (May 1931), pp. 637-46.

[22]Ruby Cohn, *Samuel Beckett: The Comic Gamut* (New Brunswick, N.J.: Rutgers University Press, 1962), p. 72. Jacqueline Hoefer, "Watt," *Perspective* (Autumn 1959), p. 172.

[23]For the Jewish aspect see the *New York Telephone Directory, Manhattan 1976-77* (New York, 1976), p. 1306. Also under "Spero," p. 1305. The Greek root of Spiro also appears in such Greek names as Spironis, Spridcs, etc.

[24]C. M. Matthews, *English Surnames* (New York: Scribner's, 1967), p. 216. Professor Tindall in Beckett suggests an interpretation which represents another interesting possibility. According to him, Watt is derived from the Anglo-Saxon of even earlier times in which it meant "know." Such as in "Ic ne wat" ("I do not know") or "Ic watt" ("I know"), pp. 17-18. On one symbolic level the name Watt implies knowledge of the useless quest for knowledge. It is very possible that Beckett chose the name with that aspect in mind as well.

[25]Matthews, p. 338. Charles W. Bardsley, *Englisy Surnames* (1889, rpt. Rutland, Vt. 1968), p. 451, considers that the name Nott or Knott may be synonymous with "shorn" since to have a "nothead" was to have the hair closely cropped all around the head. He quotes Chaucer as using the term "not-hed" and Shakespeare using it as "nott-pated" on a number of occasions.

Was Beckett aware of this possibility, known already via Bardsley's well-known work in the 19th century? On the surface it seems to have no application to his Knott. But, then, one can always indulge in Wattian speculations and come up with twelve solutions.

[26]Roland Barthes. S/Z (New York: Hill and Wang, 1974), pp. 61-62.

27*Watt*, p. 249-250.

28*Ibid.*, p. 58.

29Cohn, *Beckett*, pp. 70-71.

30*Watt*, p. 166.

31Barnard, *Beckett*, p. 24.

32Cohn, *Beckett*, pp. 82-83. See also Germaine Brée, "The Strange World of Beckett's 'grands articulés,' " in *Samuel Beckett Now: Critical Approaches to His Novels, Poetry, and Plays*, ed. Melvin J. Friedman (Chicago and London: University of Chicago Press, 1970), pp. 75-76.

33*Watt*, pp. 249-250.

34Samuel Beckett, *Our Exagmination Round his Factification for Incamination of Work in Progress* (Paris: Shakespeare and Co., 1929), p. 3.

35*Watt*, p. 73.

36*Ibid.*, p. 48.

37*Ibid.*, p. 58.

Chapter III

Plot

a) *The Illusion of* Watt *as a Simply Plotted or Plotless Novel*

Conventional criticism has struggled in vain to unravel the mystery of *Watt*'s plot. No wonder, for it appears in turn simplistic, formless, chaotic, circular, illogical with a minimum of action sequence. Some parts, such as Arthur's tale, seem to be grafted on. The time sequences of the four parts are reversible. No clearly identifiable plot structure can be unearthed since everything appears to be deceptive. One critic, G. C. Barnard, has valiantly traced the sequence of the narration for us without being able to discover a plot in this "strange tale."[1]

All this is highly confusing to the orderly critical mind accustomed as it is to seeking plot as one of the fundamentals of Western novels and drama. We do not need to recite the numerous definitions of plot. They all amount to the same. In the traditional sense of the novel, plot is the artificial machinery producing a series of coincidences and problems which, in the end, are resolved. A vital link is conflict. The speed with which these incidents are manufactured varies. In the picaresque novel of the 18th century the sweep is broad and often leisurely. In Balzac's novels, especially in *Père Goriot, Cousine Bette* and *Cousin Pons*—probably among the most brilliantly plotted novels of the 19th century—the speed is demonic. In writing of this caliber, nothing appears manufactured. Everything grows logically from the previous incident as well as from the characters and setting. Even the most outrageous reversal appears natural. The resolution of the entire novel appears unassailable. The end—whatever the ending may be—could not have happened any other way.

Conversely, the structure of *Watt*'s plot is like the visage of a sphinx. It obeys none of the traditionally accepted norms. Moreover, those critics who have discerned some essential ingredients of *Watt*'s plot are confronted by a contradiction. If the plot of *Watt* is chaotic and formless then how can it be circular at the same time? Obviously, there exists an irreconcilable difference here. Therefore, it may not be a coincidence that various critics propound only one aspect of the plot. For instance, Ruby Cohn sees *Watt* as plotless, Hesla sees chaos reflected in form while Federman opts for the circular shape. None delves deeply and none attempts to synthesize these contradictions. It is to be noted that in our linguistic study of the characters and their conceptual implications we have already contributed to a solution of the problem on one dimension.

One senses also a slight air of bewilderment on the part of the critics who proceed chronologically from *Murphy* to *Watt*. *Murphy* does have the semblance of a traditional plot. It moves forward in linear as well as temporal sequence and it displays the traditional staged events which seem plausible. For instance, the business of the gas jet contraption which finally undoes Murphy is the traditional clean resolution. Simultaneously, it constitutes a piece of pure stage-craft. But how does *Watt* end? Does it have a resolution? Could the end be the beginning, in the sense of T. S. Eliot's famous phrase? We posed the question differently at the end of the first chapter by injecting a potential thematic implication. In other words, is Knott's establishment the same as the mental institution near the race course in Dublin's outskirts? This would clearly be the result of a circular plot. The fact that this question is posed hypothetically is the direct result of Beckett's technique as far as the construction of the plot is concerned. Everything about it appears deceptive and creates illusions which lead various observers to fasten on to particular aspects. The major illusion that Beckett produces concerns the absence of a plot or its existence as a mere embryo. It is therefore not surprising that critics have abandoned this area of investigation and devoted themselves primarily to thematic studies and interpretation.

Any structural analysis of *Watt* must come to terms with this puzzle. Actually, it is no puzzle at all, although the process of unearthing a plot structure may be laborious. A good deal has already been fore-shadowed in the previous chapter. The various character structures and sub-structures do not stand by themselves amidst the apparent chaos or formlessness. They are related to a plot—not of the conventional sort as will be demonstrated—and they occupy a specific location in this relationship. For instance, the so-called extraneous inserts of various accounts are carefully crafted. They are not coincidental. Certainly they are not designed to produce interludes of relaxation for the reader, swamped as such a reader may be by the grim hopelessness of the human existence manifested here. This thematic implication or the glimpse of a thematic aspect is itself carefully crafted and is made possible by the structure of the plot. Thus if, as it appears to many, very little happens, then one level of the plot has produced that impression. If on the other hand, the situation regarding *Watt* seems to be circular, this, too, has been carefully designed. One can spin out various possibilities on the impressions the plot creates. Just as in the previous chapter various linguistic relations and structural possibilities could be played out almost indefinitely.

Plot and linguistic structures appear as deceptive as the colors of a chameleon. What appears simple or seems fairly simple to interpret suddenly acquires a variety of meanings as one takes a second glance. This tells us at once that the relationship between the complex character structures and the plot is not coincidental. In fact, they are related and very closely so. Their shifts, twists and turns are mutually produced. Moreover, they are mutually produced even if, thanks to Beckett's stagecraft (I am using the term deliberately), spatial and temporal elements are deliberately reversed or counter-reversed. The classic instance, as was noted before, is the third section in which Sam, as a fellow inmate of Watt in the insane asylum, acts as a lucid narrator. Before, the problem was posed in terms of character, character structure and structural relationship, although we threw out a strong hint that considerations of plotting were present. Of course, they are present even though the reader, including the critical reader, may be confused. It is easy to ascribe Beckett's motivation in this respect to gamesmanship—or to carelessness. If one takes that attitude, then one can dismiss it as an insignificant element. If one studies it structurally, as we are about to do, then it appears as a very serious experiment, as a matter of fact, of a philosophical nature. As such it is linked at once with the element of theme. If Sam, the madman, is giving us a surprisingly lucid account of Watt, while at the same time recognizing that this account of Watt is subjective because other persons might produce different versions of Knott, then this opens for us an endless hall of mirrors as in a movie by Resnais or Kurasawa. In short, is a definite account of an event, a person, or an entire era possible? Aren't there endless possibilities all expressed in innumerable points of view? Is reality multilayered, multi-faceted, multi-dimensional, multi-colored to the nth degree? Is reality an incomprehensible endless puzzle told by an idiot?

So we see at once that a device which appears to others either as a joke or of no consequence, is actually a carefully designed plot structure opening up various thematic possibilities. Yet all these possibilities, in the single instance cited, are hidden by the deceptiveness, rather camouflage, of what appears as a simple plot or no plot at all. This illusion is like a cone. The top is hardly visible, the base is broad and massive.

b) *Analysis of the Linear Structure with Thematic Implications*

In the first section of the novel we find some Dublin citizens engaged in chit-chat when the strange figure of Watt appears getting off a tram and walking towards the station. Certain remarks are made by these people concerning Watt, his background, and strange behavior. Then the scene shifts as Watt takes a train, meets the fanatic journalist Spiro and finally gets off. During his walk from the station he encounters Lady McCann who throws a stone at him which fortunately strikes only his hat. Watt continues and finally arrives at his destination, Knott's house. He enters and meets a servant named Arsene who proceeds to give him a very lengthy briefing. When Arsene disappears, Watt is ready to assume his new servant duties.

Briefly, this is the spine of the linear sequential structure in the first part. Despite the language which envelops it, especially in Arsene's long monologue, what transpires makes sense. To be sure, not much has transpired in the sixty-four closely-printed pages that comprise that part. All that Beckett truly gives us is a train trip, a walk and a long stationary monologue with a mysterious servant.

Actually much happens in relationship to later events. Every part of the linear sequence, as depicted above, has a counterpart in the final and fourth section even though the sequence may be reversed and even though the details may be slightly changed. Structurally, this can be demonstrated as follows:

Part I	*Part IV*
chorus	chorus
walk	walk
Arsene	Micks
violence	violence
train ride	train ride
to knott	from Knott

It must be immediately obvious that these counterparts are not exact replicas. They are merely corresponding sub-structures of the plot. Thus the people of the chorus in Part I are not the same people in Part IV with the exception of Lady McCann. But as examples of typical Dubliners they fulfill their role as objects of Beckett's satire. Moreover, they are the outer world around Watt which is unchanging in spite of his various journeys and experiences. We shall turn to this important thematic point from time to time. Arsene leaves, Micks arrives. In either case this is a signal for Watt. In one instance, he commences his employment in Knott's house. In the other he finishes it. In part I the violence consists of a stone thrown by Lady McCann. In Part IV Watt collides with a door thrown by Mr. Nolan. In Part I the stone thrown merely strikes Watt's hat and therefore causes no laceration of his skin. No blood flows (Watt's skins heals poorly). In Part IV Watt is knocked out and blood flows.

There is no need to delve further into these corresponding sub-structures. Those that we have omitted are obvious, or so delicate that they would distract us from the major hypothesis of the plot. Suffice it to say at this point that these correspondences are so constructed as to result in what appears to be a closing circle. Yet we must immediately insert a warning. It is not to be inferred from this that the entire plot is circular, but only the outer shell. It is like the ring around Jupiter. What happens on the surface or the interior of the planet may be an entirely different matter. So it is here.

What is the purpose of this parallel plot construction of parts I and IV? The reader of Part I has, of course, no idea of the surprising development to come in Part IV. In the conventional sense, he or she might expect a clean resolution. In fact, in the vast majority of conventional novels one half-consciously perceives the ending in advance. Usually the problem is solved by the hero or heroine. Beckett has thrown that mechanical convention overboard. And with it he has achieved surprise.

Of course, as we noted in the last chapter, he has planted some clues in Arsene's philosophical monologue which Watt, as Arsene expects, does not understand. Watt will fail. Yet this is so delicately seeded that the most careful reader does not fathom how Watt will fail. Yet the exact manner of failure is subject to speculation. Isn't failure an attribute of Watt which exists from the moment we meet him and which is immediately discerned by Arsene? In other words, given the character structure of Watt and the structured condition of the world around him it can be posited, thematically, that failure is a permanent condition of Watt, if not of life. Yet Beckett's construction of the outer plot cleverly obscures this. We do not find it. Therefore, our surprise.

Another overriding condition is the fact that the linear sequence of the outer shell is simultaneously bent into a circle. I stress the term "simultaneously" because each sequence, linear or circular, exists independently and yet as one entity. What deviates also converges. Opposites meet in a synthesis.

> of the coming to
> of the being at
> of the going from
> Knott's habitat
>
> of the long way
> of the short stay

of the going back home
the way he had come 2

In the second part (Chapter II) the linear sequence becomes somewhat complex. Watt starts performing his menial duties which are interrupted at intervals by various mysterious occurrences. The piano tuners Gall arrive. Watt speculates about Knott's dogs and the movements of his fellow servant Erskine. His search for a medium of communication between Erskine and Knott leads him finally, after some complicated attempts, into Erskine's room where he spies a strange picture depicting a black circle on white ground with a blue dot inside but not in the center. Dot and circle seem to be moving, each in search of the other. The circle also has a break which can serve as an entrance or an exit. Watt subsequently recalls his strange affair with Mrs. Gorman. The part ends with the arrival of a stranger who resembles Arsene and Erskine in posture. The stranger is Arthur.

Superficially very little happens in part II. It could be summarized in two sentences: Watt works—Watt speculates.

The mere placement of these short phrases underscores linear sequence but also progression. Watt moves from work or rather through work to speculation. Work begets speculation. It is a very special Wattian speculation which consists of discovering problems that have to be solved even though no problems may be present in the first place for anyone else. Moreover, having posed the problem Watt can think of several co-existing solutions which, in turn, can be opposed by several objections. Such fantastic mental activity is illustrated in the case of Knott's mythical dog and the story of the Lynch family. In both cases the subjects under investigation multiply endlessly.

The Wattian brain, once unleashed on its compulsive Cartesian pursuit, cannot be stopped. Its rational machinery has run wild. Thus the actionless plot is superseded by the endless action of mental lucubrations.

Hugh Kenner has done some pathbreaking work in interpreting the meaning of the endless number sequences which occur so prominently in the later trilogy yet find their initial reflection in *Watt,* especially in the song Watt hears on his way to Knott. These number sequences are analogous to Watt's endless speculations and, in fact, to his fictional approach, although Kenner does not examine their relationship to the plot. On example will suffice:

$$1 + \cfrac{1}{2 + \cfrac{1}{2 + \cfrac{1}{2 + \cfrac{1}{2 + \dots}}}}{}^3$$

This is the classic Pythagorean problem with its square root of two which trails off into meaninglessness. One does not have to delve further into mathematics to recognize the form of Watt's speculation to which this corresponds. Watt cannot get away from this serial and he cannot get away from the square root. One problem solved produces another problem still to be solved and so on. It ends in irrationality.

Beckett has therefore prepared the reader for Watt's mental breakdown. At the same time he has also given us an excellent thematic sample. These irrational number systems exist in the world side by side with other systems of a more rational sort, for instance, plane geometry. Suffice it to say at this point that what has been called the "most irrational of all numbers,"[4] the square root of minus one, is linked with relativity physics, one of the dominant scientific influences in the twentieth century. At any rate, we shall examine these philosophic considerations regarding Beckett's view of the world in the next chapter.

What is more important at the moment is the fact that Beckett's plot at the end of the second part has entered a state of crisis. By showing us how and why Watt is going mad the linear sequential structure faces collapse. Watt and his actions have become irrational. How to continue artistically and to reach the desired symmetries of the outer circle of the plot in the concluding fourth part? In a stroke of pure genius in conception Beckett solves the problem in the crucial third part. He performs an act of antithesis by reversing time, space, even language.

c) *Antithesis—Spatial and Temporal Reversal*

The climax builds in Part III—foreshadowing Beckett's later dramatic creations. Watt is now in a mental institution—or what appears as such—where he gradually deteriorates. It must be noted at once that this situation, however, freed from the constraints of linear sequential structure, cannot be fixed in exact temporal or chronological terms. As was noted before, this aspect is one of the most intriguing of the novel. It appears to occur while Watt is in Knott's employment yet it could also have happened after he left Knott. In fact, it could even have happened before he ever came to work for Knott. Everything is relative and "all is possible." In short, everything that was related before—and afterwards— could result from the irrational fantasies of Knott which he experiences in the asylum. Knott and his establishment may never have existed.

Moreover, what we call plot no longer quite applies. The narrator is now Sam, the fellow inmate, who relates what he has been told by Watt. We are now in an endless hallway of mirrors. To quote again Hugh Kenner:

> Beckett invariably backs the mode he is practising into its last cor-
> ner, and is most satisfied if he can render further performance in
> that mode, by him impossible. Every game is an end game. If fiction,
> for instance, mirrors the minutiae of life, then there stretches before
> every fiction-writer an infinity of possible novels: more various even,
> if that be possible, than life, since after a time the novels themselves
> commence to interbreed. But if the series can be made not to diverge
> but to converge toward some limit, then very close to that limit we
> shall find the Beckettian writer amassing his negligible increments.
> Fiction, for instance, will converge if narrator M1 and his story are
> inventions of narrator M2 who in turn . . . . [5]

Unfortunately Kenner does not pursue this point and instead devotes himself to more interpretation of number sequences, especially as they apply to the other novels. Yet the last part of the statement quoted is extremely pertinent in our case. "M2," Sam who has replaced the omniscient author of the first two parts, gives us admittedly only one version of Watt's adventures in Knott's establishment. Yet this is sufficient to carry the novel forward. Moreover, it infuses the entire account with the delicious sensation experienced by the reader that everything related is nonsense. After all, the new narrator is a madman. How can we trust him?

Thematically, this is extremely important. We are presented in this era of relativity with the proposition that all "truth" is relative. Truth can be uttered by a madman as well as by a sane person—yet both may be wrong. Does truth exist? Can it even be grasped?

I mentioned before that the concept of plot no longer quite applies in this new situation. It, too, is relative. In this fluid and chaotic situation in which everything is possible, even a god-like metamorphosis of Knott (expressed as one of Watt's later "fancies"), there are still rocks of the plot sticking out of treacherous waters. They appear just after Sam's description of Watt's decline. He inverts words and sentences. He walks backwards. Moreover, Sam's hearing has begun to fail. It is high time to pump fresh air into the story or apply a new turn of the screw because the story is in danger of sinking into visible gibberish. Obviously, if the sounds of the inverted language of Watt can no longer be understood by an increasingly deaf Sam the page has to be filled by scraps of words. At this point Arthur and Graves step onto the scene. Graves complaining about his impotence launches Arthur into what may be the funniest segment of the novel.

Yet for our purposes its content, which has been indicated before, is not as important as the plotting or the structures of the fragmented plot of this part. In brief, Graves fulfills the function of launching Arthur theatrically. In turn, Arthur who always absents himself from Knott and always returns once again calls attention to the chief mystery of Knott which we may have forgotten in the meantime. After all, the Graves/Arthur exchange about "bando" and the remarkable satire of academe which follows have taken up exactly thirty pages. So Arthur restores the balance. We plunge into Watt's final hallucinations or perhaps visions regarding Knott.

There is little question that Part III is the most remarkable section of the novel. It is also the most difficult. Certainly as far as our study of plot is concerned, for this is the core of the planet and all is molten lava boiling or perhaps cooling. We are far from the outer rings of the plot. All is chaos and yet there is some order. Certainly some conceptual order for the reader. For instance, if Sam could utter only gibberish the account would be unreadable. Beckett, as Kenner rightly suggests, strains for the utmost limit. Dimensions of time, setting, language, character and movement exist simultaneously while being in flux. For instance, poetic language shifts to inverted sentences which sound like gibberish, then shifts to satire about academic life, and so on. At each stage there is a decline of language followed by an ascent. Just as at the end of the part Watt walks backward away from Sam through the hole in the underbrush towards his own pavilion. Thus the poetic language at the end corresponds to poetic language at the beginning where, incidentally, the garden of the asylum which is the crucial setting, its shrubbery and Watt's strange walk are introduced. So, once again, we find a certain symmetry or correspondence in structure as we found by comparing Parts I and IV. It appears there is an inner ring being formed, not a full-fledged structure, rather a secondary sub-structure in formation on the cooling outer fringes of the chaotic interior.

The attempt to study the plot structure—or its traces—in Part III is not easy, considering its shifts from chaos to structure and back to chaos. Yet compared to these labors Beckett's task of conception, not to speak of execution, is infinitely bigger. For in this part the themes and their strands, even substrands, have taken over. Content has become form. For instance, if the modern rationalism of Western civilization is headed for dissolution or chaos then this is expressed here in Watt's breakdown as a result of compulsive rational speculations which eventually turn irrational. Yet this is only one major reflection of Beckett's tenets. It is therefore quite clear how difficult it has been to express all this without driving the reader into stupor. In short, how do you picture a nervous breakdown and a schizophrenic state of an individual which may on a cosmic scale mirror the irrationality and chaos of our modern world? No one in the many disciplines derived from traditional psychology has equalled Beckett's accomplishments in this respect.

d) *Analysis of the Cyclical Structure*

In the preceding sections of this study stress has been laid upon uncovering cyclical qualities in the plot's structures. However, it was also pointed out that the cyclical or circular is by no means the predominant mode. There is no predominant mode. The circular is very visible. It serves either as an adornment swirling around the planet of Beckettian creation or as a corrective girdle to prevent a rupture as in Part III. The circle is not perfect. Just as in the painting in Erskine's room there is a break in the circle so there is a corresponding break in the hedge of the asylum's garden through which Watt appears and eventually disappears.

Moreover, a linear sequence, as in plot, can be bent into the circular through synthesis. The opposite is also possible. In fact, one can apply this to other structures and other possibilities. Watt's language, for instance, has become so inverted that its words and sequences have almost performed a somersault. Yet in Part IV he resumes his normal speech.

Of course, Part IV represents a reversal of time sequence just as Part III represents a reversal of the same sequence as far as Part II is concerned. This has given the critics a good deal of trouble, accustomed as they are to dealing with what could be described as an "orderly" block of time. To make matters worse, there are some reversals of time sequences within the parts themselves and sometimes they occur very abruptly indeed. Characters seem to fly backwards and forwards within the mass of time without order. Time is chaotic.

Of course, we know that in the Beckettian universe time is relative. This is precisely one of the causes of Watt's breakdown, for his demonic rationality was unable to adjust itself to this elasticity.

> One of the first things that Watt learned by these means was that Mr Knott sometimes arose late and retired early, and sometimes rose very late and retired very early, and sometimes did not rise at all, nor at all retire, for who can retire who does not arise? What interested Watt here was this, that the earlier Mr Knott rose the later he

retired, and that the later he rose the earlier he retired. But between the hour of his rising and the hour of his retiring there seemed no fixed correlation, or one so abstruse that it did not exist, for Watt.[6]

This passage goes on to tell us that Watt realized that there was no difference between Knott's time of rising and retiring; in fact, Knott never seemed to sleep or to be awake. The activity of rising and retiring seemed to be connected with an entirely different state.

We have here the first signs of the impending breakdown. Watt seeks a "fixed correlation" for certain phenomena in time which may have existed only in his brain. Immediately thereafter he plunges into his famous speculations concerning Knott's meal habits and the dogs.

The above quoted passage has another idea implanted which calls attention to the circular. If there is no difference between time elements or certain physical states, such as rising and retiring, then existence is circular.

Watt later has an inkling of this when he speculates on the meaning of the mysterious picture in Erskine's room. "Yes, nothing changed in Mr Knott's establishment, because nothing remained, and nothing came or went, all was a coming and a going."[7] Therefore at the end of the novel the "coming to" or the "going from" Knott's house is the same for Watt.

By now it is very obvious that the circular is more than a plot structure. It is an expression of Beckett's point of view which constantly forms the structure while being formed by it.

Yet the circle is not perfect. Its opening enables the circumference to bend or straighten until it reaches the straight line. In fact, the line may be broken. The blue dot in Erskine's picture is not the center. Both the black circumference and the dot seem to be constantly moving in a search—or what appears to Watt as a search. There is movement, otherwise all existence would be at a standstill. Ceaseless movement in various directions. Chaotic movement in which the conventional rules of physics seem to be constantly broken. This, too, is reflected in the structure which in Part II and certainly in Part III is in constant flux. Can this chaos of movement overwhelm the circles? No. It is barely contained, threatens to flow out of the circle's opening and then immediately flows back to resume the process all over again. To sum up: existence is chaotic and circular at the same time. Form rules chaos but chaos also rules form. And in Beckett's hand the plot structure reflects that idea.

e) *Conceptual Implications: Narrative Prose Versus Stagecraft Dialogue*

In *Watt* Beckett for the first time attempts to take the novel to its limits by performing the very dangerous act of being what Kenner calls a "rope dancer." The novels that succeeded *Watt* accelerated the processes described as typical in *Watt*. Beckett the novelist seemed to be possessed by a drive similar to his character's. He gradually threw overboard all the elements of the novel until there was scarcely a novel in the traditional sense. Finally, between the late 1940's and the late 1950's he turned to playwriting as a craft. He had found a more suitable artistic medium.

This turn is definitely foreshadowed in *Watt*, specifically in its language.

The traditional critic who peruses *Watt*, or attempts to peruse it, may be repelled by certain aspects which violate his norms. Among them would be deviant syntax, sentence structure, punctuation, and strange spelling, endless repetition and such other phenomena as meaningless phrases, poems, songs or tables imbedded in the text. However, the chief objection would probably be directed against the endless sentences run together with hardly any punctuation, sometimes in an annoying repetitive pattern for several pages.

On the other hand, any fairly sensitive person whose ear is attuned to the English language by reading aloud these closely printed pages will discover the poetry of music, or in a typically Beckettian reversal, the music of poetry.

From Beckett's prose, one derives an emotional impact, an aural impact which eventually becomes visual at the same time. Certainly anyone plowing through the scenes in the garden of the sanatorium obtains the visual feeling of irrationality. It is a far deeper mental image than that furnished by a TV special on a mental institution and its horrors. After all, we have the commentator's first-hand experience before us. Sam can calmly—and at times emotionally—explain how he accommodates Watt in his strange backward walk or plays games with him.

Beckett has also furnished us with the aids of poetic inserts and music that critics find offensive because they seem to have no place in the well-made traditional novel. These devices are obviously inserted to heighten our reading experiences and also our understanding of the text because they contain, as has been shown, important clues.

Yet opposed to this are some sections of absolutely first-rate dialogue. samples of which have been quoted before. The dialogue is terse, compact, accurate as far as the characters are concerned, and infused at times with other meanings which take it beyond the speaker's plane or dimension. Thus it is clear and puzzling at the same time. In that sense it anticipates to an astonishing degree the dialogue employed by Harold Pinter in his plays where characters while talking to each other simultaneously seem to talk past each other.

How is one to account for the dichotomy existing between massive blocks of narrative prose which tend towards the lyrical, even outright music by a repetitive cadence on the one hand and the economical sparseness of dialogue on the other.

The dialogue at times acts as a powerful propellant in advancing the action. Dialogue is also employed when Beckett commences one of his dizzying shifts. Arsene's address is also basically dialogue.

The very power of the dialogue points to strengths and weaknesses in the prose. The philosophical concepts, the many planes they represent, the clash of dimensions, the psychological tunings and shades involved in the character structures as well as in the plot and the necessary physical descriptions are attributable to the kind of narrative prose employed by Beckett. At the same time, the speculations with their endless mathematical serial progressions and the investigations of useless minutiae which are the characteristic obsession of Watt can also be expressed that way. Or perhaps only in this fashion. How else, other than in prose, can one describe Watt's mad speculations regarding the vast progeny of the Lynch family and its twenty-eight members?

Yet there is a weakness inherent in this prosaic mode. Its concepts function only when we deal with obsessed characters as in *Watt* and the trilogy. But these characters—and specifically Watt— must be analyzed and explained not through direct description from the outside but by conveying their subjective thought processes. Moreover, given Beckett's thematic approach with its stress on relativity, various narrators may be employed.

All this is successfully carried out in *Watt.* I do not hold with those who assert the novel is a failure. On the contrary, it opens up immense vistas and techniques for novelistic use, provided one does not write oneself into a corner. This danger is discernible in *Watt.* So is the danger of incomprehensibility in the language and Beckett's experiments with it. It seems a foregone conclusion that after *Watt* Beckett if he persisted with his linguistic experiments would take a drastic step. He did. He abandoned his native language. When French could not take the strain, he abandoned the novel.

There is the rub. In spite of these peregrinations one thing remained more or less unchanged, dialogue. Later Beckett could get rid of plot, of character, of setting, but he could not get rid of dialogue, which remained powerful. Finally, he jettisoned the ballast or prose altogether. A playwright was not born. Beckett as a playwright was always present, especially in Watt. This is the reason why I have stressed theatrical terminology.

It might be asked why Beckett did not write *Watt* as a play. Could he not have expressed the cosmic panorama of *Watt* in his marvelous dialogue? The highly speculative answer to this must be that he could not have. Not at this stage of his life. His creative instincts were still unable to absorb his vast learning, his philosophies, his investigations and compress them into poetry and drama. It must be remembered that these two forms are the literary archetypes of humanity. Prose narration is essentially modern and rational. Beckett thus was forced to travel backwards artistically to arrive at the right medium without changing his philosophical beliefs.

This is the ultimate conceptual implication as far as the literary techniques of *Watt* are concerned: the seeds of *Waiting for Godot, Endgame* and *Krapp's Last Tape* are sprouting.

Notes

[1] Barnard, *op. cit.*, p. 26.

[2] *Watt, op, cit.*, pp. 249-250.

[3] Kenner, *Samuel Beckett, op. cit.*, p. 106.

[4] Barnard, p. 18.

[5] Kenner, p. 105.

[6] *Watt*, p, 86.

[7] *Ibid.*, pp. 131-132.

Chapter IV

Philosophical and Aesthetic Concepts

In the preceding pages we have attempted to perform an ana-
tomical operation on *Watt*. The objective of this exercise was to lay
bare the network of structures and substructures on various technical
literary levels which infuse the work, to show the various structural
relationships with their thematic/conceptual implications.

This process could be compared to the dissection of an orange.
We have peeled the fruit, broken up the various segments, studied
their composition, position, relationship including the presence of
the pips and drawn certain conclusions. Yet we have not grappled
with the ultimate question. Why is it an orange and not a cherry?
After all, the creative source of both, fruit trees, do not so differ in
appearance. Why does one tree produce an orange and another
cherries? Why does one author produce *Watt* and another *Portnoy's
Complaint?* In the case of the fruits the element of climate among
other factors suggests itself. In the case of literary compositions a
host of such elements suggests itself, ranging from personality to
nationality. In fact, we have tried briefly in a literary sense to answer
the question about the strong dramaturgical elements in *Watt* and
why Beckett at the time was not able to cast *Watt* in the form of a
play. On the other hand, why didn't Beckett write a philosophical
treatise on *Watt?* We shall try to answer that question in our conclusions. Yet it is clear in general terms that we grapple with the intellectual world of the creator of *Watt*, with the metaphysical and philosophical elements which form *Watt*, its structural edifice and aesthetic conception which is expressed in the point of view of the narrators, omniscient or otherwise, and various characters.

The point of view, the vantage point from which Beckett presents the actions in *Watt*, is just as complex as the actions themselves. It has been nurtured by an amalgam of various influences ranging from pre-Socratic philosophy and Eastern religious concepts to contemporary scientific and linguistic theory. Nevertheless, Beckett does not present us with a unified philosophical system which underlies his point of view or those of his characters. Yet this complex mosaic of thought determines the structural conception of the novel.

Therefore *Watt* cannot be judged by traditional literary standards alone. To the dismay of conventional critics such purely "literary" efforts result in chaotic and fanciful interpretations which provide no satisfaction and only reinforce the mystery of *Watt* and Beckett's other novels. To judge as formidable a thinker and literary artist as Beckett without examining the intellectual conceptions behind his novels is a fruitless and shallow enterprise. The following analysis will delve into those regions which few critics have so far visited.

a) *Watt in the World of Flux and Opposites*

If one were to name one of the chief characteristics of *Watt* one could simply sum it up as restless change. Everything undergoes constant transformation through antithesis and synthesis: language, character structures, plot structures. In the universe of *Watt* it is as if innumerable formations of atomic and sub-atomic particles collide, fuse, absorb each other while their new shapes or descendants continue an endless dance. There is a constant coming and going and a constant becoming. And yet—curiously—no one and nothing dies. No one, in the biblical phrase, "slept with his fathers." Moreover, entire generations are described in their genealogical descent as is the case with Knott's servants; yet the vertical movement turns into a horizontal cavalcade. Their places are taken by others and the parade continues as if nothing had happened. In fact, as we noted repeatedly, it appears that in a circular dimensional sense there is no beginning and no ending. Even time is subject to this process. In fact, it has ceased to exist in an earthly sense so that it appears not only as an illusion but a delusion.

This process of constant flux could have come straight from Heraclitus and is embodied in his thesis that the opposition and identity of contraries are the causal condition of existence.

> It is the same in us to be what is living and to be what is dead, awake and asleep, young and old; for, by change, one is the other and by change the other, in its turn, is the former.[1]

Or, in other terms, the famous saying that he who dips into a river "will not dip twice in the same water."[2]

> The discordant . . . agrees with itself—a harmony of opposite tensions, as in the bow or the lyre . . . . Things which are cut in opposite directions . . . fit together. The fairest harmony is born of things different and discord is what produces all things.[3]

This part of his philosophy, a dialectic, has had a lasting influence on Western philosophical thought. It is also reflected in contemporary science.

Giordano Bruno, who was deeply influenced by Heraclitus, fashioned a similar thesis by describing the figures of constellations being changed to their opposites. He also cast some of his conclusions in the form of striking paradoxes which recall the aphorisms of Heraclitus. Beckett refers to Bruno's treatment of "identifiable contraries" in his supremely important early essay on Joyce[4] and declares that Bruno had a great influence on Vico's conception of the cyclical patterns of history. Beckett saw the principle of "identified contraries" in striking terms which echo Heraclitus:

> There is no difference between the smallest possible chord and the smallest possible arc, no difference between the infinite circle and the straight line. The maxima and minima of particular contraries are one and indifferent. Minimal heat equals minimal cold. Consequently transmutations are circular. The principle (minimum) of one contrary takes its movement from the principle (maximum) of another . . . . Maximal speed is a state of rest. The maximum of corruption . . . is generation.[5]

Even though Heraclitus is clearly the progenitor of some of Bruno's conceptions, he is not mentioned in Beckett's essay. Nevertheless, we have ample evidence of his impact on Beckett's work. One scholar, Professor Sighle Kennedy, has done some fruitful work in this area which is virtually virgin territory as far as the criticism is concerned. She has traced Heraclitus' influence in some of Beckett's early stories and especially in *Murphy*.[6]

We have noted in *Watt*'s case Heraclitus' overall influence in general terms especially as far as the tempo and flavor of the action is concerned. All is unceasing change yet that change produces constant movement which is not always evident on first reading especially if one gets immured in one of the long passages. However, a special effort, heightened by the act of reading aloud, produces an altogether different impression.

The prime example in this respect is, of course, Arsene's "short statement" to Watt which ends abruptly with, "goodnight." It is not only a philosophical statement by Arsene filtered through the prism of his character, but at the same time expresses the overall Beckettian viewpoint regarding the universe of Watt. The key word in that passage is "change."

Arsene describes that one afternoon he became aware that a change had taken place. He is unable to define precisely what had changed except that it was the "existence off the ladder." It might be noted that this phrase and the following "Do not come down the ladder, Ifor, I haf taken it away"[7] have been seized upon by some to construct a hypothesis regarding Beckett's opposition to the linguistic doctrines of the Austro/British philosopher Wittgenstein, but this is merely blowing up a trifle. One of Beckett's puns, which need not detain us.

However, Arsene illustrates his belief that a change had taken place in a series of metaphors. These depict changes in various conditions ranging from inanimate nature and the seasons to persons. Incidentally, in some of these passages the word "flux" is introduced to add a further Heraclitean identification. The presence of Bruno's "identified contraries" and the process of transformation and synthesis of such opposite tendencies is clearly shown. Most important of all, is the conclusion that all this represents a perennial process which is really without significance—except to a philosopher. ·

These passages are strikingly beautiful, some are among the best and most poetic in the novel, such as the movement of the grains of sand on a dune. Others delight because of their imaginative coarseness. To wit, the digestive practices of maid Mary.

Arsene's philosophical conception of the universe, which can be classified as part cosmological and partly ontological is beyond Watt's understanding. Arsene knows it. Watt is not only a compulsive speculator but a speculator *par excellence* in the tradition of Descartes' *"Cogito ergo sum."* Watt's thinking is the cause of his existence or to put it in slightly different terms, Watt's speculations not only prove his existence to himself but to the world.

This is, of course, a complete reversal of ancient Greek philosophy as Heisenberg has brilliantly demonstrated.[8] In ancient Greek philosophy the starting point was a fundamental principle or substance. Descartes aimed at a fundamental knowledge. One of the dangerous consequences of the Cartesian philosophy was the tendency to think of animals, plants, and finally men as mere machines whose behavior was completely determined by material causes. Descartes also contributed to the spirit, already evident in the Renaissance, of thought in linear terms which ultimately culminated in the 19th century amelioristic conception of infinite progress.

It is interesting to note here that Watt in his philosophical speculations not only progresses linearly, but is concerned with "things," another important aspect of Cartesianism. He is totally uninterested in abstract fundamental principles. Therefore we find him dwelling on various speculations about meals, telephones, bells, pots, rooms, keys, entrances, etc. Yet something does not work. He not only arrives at varying solutions to his imaginary problems but also registers objections. There is a strong hint of the modern probability principle (developed by Heisenberg, Schroedinger and other), but Watt's mind cannot conceive of such a possibility. So he goes mad.

Still Watt eventually and inevitably becomes enmeshed in the eternal process of change and is changed by it. But if Watt is changed, as had been predicted by the seer Arsene who consciously experienced change in himself, so the accompanying structure of the narration is shifted. The madness of Watt, which is accompanied by varying changes of the other characters, especially of Knott, has to be made intelligible and not for plot purposes alone. So Sam is produced. For some reason he keeps a journal in which he notes down what Watt tells him about his stay in Knott's house. We have previously examined the curious structure of the subjective and one-sided nature of Watt's account—which Sam stresses—and of the irony that this account is given to us by a fellow inmate in a mental institution. So this is Watt's view of what happened to him filtered through Sam's subjective view. However, Sam's observations of Watt's speech and other behavior appear to be objective—or as far as objectivity is possible within the parameters of this universe which is constantly shifting.

We must examine other parts of the narrative structure and its shifts. In Part I we seem to be dealing with a double image of narration. On one hand there appears to be an omniscient narrator as supreme director. On the other hand, a great deal concerning Watt is either seen through the eyes of the Dublin citizens' chorus or via Arsene. So we have a multiplicity of the narrative viewpoints. These congeal in Part II into a solid structure in which there are hints of another "I," another narrator. In Part III this "I" which remains obscure is changed to "Sam" who incidentally turns out to be responsible for Part II. Part III is thus the synthesis as well as the climax wherein all narrators, alleged or real, merge into "Sam." Part IV, at least the beginning portion, can be attributed to Sam as well. Then we return to the beginning with the omniscient narrator as well as the chorus. The chorus has, of course, changed. With the exception of Lady McCann, we are presented with different Dublin characters. Nevertheless, they play their assigned roles in the same fashion as the initial characters of the chorus.

There is a hint of still another possible narrator. In the so-called "addenda" we are informed that Arthur has kept a journal. This sets up an interesting conjecture. Are the parts of the novel, which cannot be attributed directly to Sam, reflections, in part or whole, of that journal? Or is the same possibility applicable even to some parts within Sam's narration? In other words, does Arthur represent still another level of narration and point of view? Or are we presented with the possibility that this dimension does not exist in the novel because Arthur's journal has been "lost" or has never been integrated into text?

Nevertheless, we can plot the changes of the narrative structure as follows:

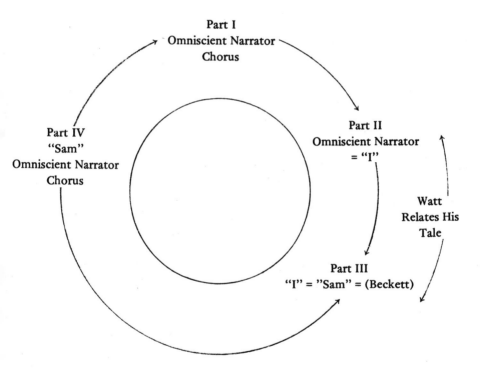

Possible Identity of Arthur and Sam

This graph enables us to solve several problems in the spirit of the Heraclitus/Bruno philosophical concepts which they reflect.

The "flux" of the narrative structure reflects simultaneously the shift in viewpoints of the various narrators employed. Yet this structure, represented by a circle, also depicts infinity. In other words, the whole process begins again.

In the second chapter we have demonstrated that the characters move from antithesis to synthesis to transformation in an endless process. In short, identifiable contraries merge, even Knott with Watt. If we apply this process of the transformation of the character structures to our graph then we may glean an interesting new dimension. Not only does the merger of Knott/Watt or Watt/Knott raise the possibility that Watt may have simply imagined Knott while working in a house where there was no Knott but that Sam and Arthur may be the same character as were indeed all the servants. In fact, Arsene, the philosopher/seer who can stand off from all this strongly hints as much to Watt.

With this suggestion in hand, we can envision Beckett's ultimate step: the fusion of narrative structure with characters reducing it finally to a single activity involving a sole character. It was all a "long wet dream" that Watt had while on the train traveling on one of his frequent journeys. Most likely after listening to Spiro and falling asleep. And then Spiro suddenly flew out the window "through the night" and Watt suddenly found himself on a road. That's when it all began .

b) *Cycles and Circles*

If Beckett said little about Bruno and was silent about Heraclitus in his essay on Joyce, he compensated by his extensive treatment of Vico and to a lesser degree of Dante. He ascribed to both of them a profound influence on Joyce's *Work in Progress.* It is obvious that the Neapolitan author of the *New Science (Nuova Scienza)* exercised a most powerful impact upon the young Beckett. This is even more remarkable because in 1929 when the essay on Joyce appeared Vico's works were available only in a few translations in the English-speaking world and the recognition of his towering stature came only in the post-World War II period. In fact, there is internal evidence in the essay which hints that Beckett read his Vico in the original Italian.

At any rate, Beckett singles out two theories of Vico which to him were revolutionary. First, the division of the development of human society into three ages, Theocratic, Heroic and Human (civilized). This, what Beckett calls "ineluctable circular progression of Society,"[9] corresponds to a matching development of language, theocratic, poetic, and philosophical. All human societies pass through this three-stage cycle and then by means of a "reflux" *(ricorso)* flow back and the process starts all over again.

Beckett devoted the bulk of his discussion on Vico to the development of language which was entirely appropriate because of its application to Joyce's work which featured daring linguistic experiments. We have quoted one such passage of Beckett in Chapter II in which he tries to show that Joyce's style is "pure Vico."

Vico's theory of historical cycles had already been foreshadowed by Polybius' "Circular movement," by Plato, Campanelli, Machiavelli and Bruno, but Beckett only credits the latter. In political terms, Vico's theory views societies as passing from barbarism back to barbarism via aristocracy, feudalism and democracy in flux and reflux while the corresponding development of language travels upward in a spiral motion.

> The mind, after traversing its course of progress, after rising from sensation successively to the imaginative and the rational universal and from violence to equity, is bound in conformity with its eternal nature to retraverse the course, to relapse into violence and sensation, and thence to renew its upward movement, to commence a reflux.[10]

Incidentally, Vico saw time also in the same motion like a sphere, but Beckett does not discuss this. He is fascinated by the flow of the historical cycle and by the flow of language. He quotes with approval Joyce's analogy between the historical theory and the circular Vico Road in Dublin: "The Vico Road goes round and round to meet where terms begin."[11]

The flux and reflux of the Viconian cycles of history fits in admirably with the philosophical framework of the Heraclitus/Bruno influence on *Watt*. As we noted in our discussion of the plot in Chapter II, it provides a sort of ring and girdle for the core where everything is in constant flux and where "contraries" meet, transfer and are reborn.

Superficially, Beckett's narrative structure is not only discontinuous but a puzzle, even chaotic, deriving from various philosophical concepts. Perhaps the best view of structure in this instance is Beckett's own explanation:

> By structural I do not mean a bold outward division, a bare skeleton for the housing of material. I mean the endless substantial variations of these three beats, and interior intertwining of these three themes into a decoration of arabesques—decoration and more than decoration.[12]

Here Beckett refers to Vico's three themes (historical and linguistic stages) and applies them to Joyce's work. But the conclusion is inevitable that he applied his version of the philosophical structure in a literary/aesthetic sense to *Watt* just as he had previously applied it to *Murphy* as Professor Kennedy has demonstrated.

Moreover, this structure is buttressed or rather refined by Beckett's view (in his work of Joyce) of Dante's tripartite Paradise, Purgatory and Hell as the counterpart of Vico's "three themes." However, Beckett devotes the thrust of his analysis to Purgatory which he finds exhibits the same structural form used by Joyce. In Purgatory there are not only "endless substantial variations" but there is "flux—progression and retrogression."[13] Ultimately in Joyce's work, there is a synthesis between the two extremes, Heaven and Hell, which influences Purgatory in a ceaseless movement which is "nondirectional or multidirectional." These extremes never congeal or stand still. They are locked in a circle of endless transformation which characterizes the purgatorial process.

"Non-directional" or "multidirectional" are not only excellent characterizations of the narrative structure in *Watt* (non-linear or discontinuous are contemporary terms) but they also apply to the characters and setting. With these Beckettian terms as guides we can examine why the characters in *Watt* are capable of what we might call in conventional literary terms "irrational" behavior as far as their movements are concerned. They float in on us, and depart and reappear in dreamlike, imprecise actions. Their actions resemble ballet movements free of the laws of gravitation, free of any specific setting, except for the chorus at the beginning of a cycle or its reflux. Ditto Watt who is the only one whose walk is minutely described. But note this: in the beginning and in the final scenes he exhibits an exaggerated manner of walking. In the middle of the novel he floats and—then reverses his walk. In fact he walks backwards in the asylum—with Sam who has adopted this manner to guide Watt. In short, the reverse process has already set in. But, then, Watt experiences a form of reflux in other aspects as well.

If the characters dance partly in chaos and ultimately in a circle, the same can be applied to the setting. The Dublin railroad station dissolves into the phantasmagoria of Knott's house where Knott eventually dissolves into an abstract principle. Moreover, inside the house and especially inside the asylum we are treated to constant shifts in setting because of flashbacks and other stories emanating from the characters. Yet these shifts are never clearly defined. They do not occur in any rational linear sequence. Neither do they dissolve as cleanly as in a film. They glide by us in an imprecise pattern, either superimposed on each other or totally disjointed and separated. The effect is that of a dream in which the elements of time and space work seemingly at random. Nevertheless, at the end we reach the railroad station. This is inevitable. The circle must return there, the reflux starts until the game begins again.

A corollary to these shifts in setting is the fluidity of spatial relationships. At times it appears as if space had been abolished or swallowed up in the novel. At the least it is very distorted. For instance, we never know where the station is, how long the initial train ride lasts or where Watt is getting off except that it must be near a race course. The latter point, incidentally, is one symbol firmly embedded—almost like a fixed point in space and therefore a teaser—because the race course is apparently near the asylum as we pointed out at the end of Chapter I. We do not know the distance from the station to Knott's house and, incredibly, we are actually very badly informed about the house itself. Its physical properties are almost magical. We do know it has an entrance door, a downstairs and an upstairs and a garden. But these items are revealed sparingly and when they appear they assume a separate existence of their own each with a special significance for Watt. Thus they are actually parts and each part is a separate world for Watt, especially Erskine's and Knott's room. Yet they do not make a house, and, because they do not, they merely interact upon each other. Ultimately, only the world of Knott's room exists and it gives way to the garden of the asylum following the dreamlike pattern of superimposed images noted before.

The asylum has several pavilions and a garden which is surrounded by a wire fence. There is also a brook. Beyond the fence is the thick, luxuriant underbrush of what may be another garden or a wood. The fence also has a hole. Now Sam, to whom we are indebted for this information is very confused about the entire layout. In terms which recall Watt's speculations, he tries to account for the strange blurred, spatial relationships which seem to be present. The fence is not a fence but part of a fence and the underbrush may actually overflow that mysterious fence and be inside the asylum's grounds. In fact, there may be two holes in the fence. Watt emerges from one hole, while Sam goes to meet him using another hole. The entire physical layout is very hazy so that we never know whether we are in an asylum or in a wood or where the pavilions are. In short, we are treated to the possibility that there is a thin line between the world of insanity inside the asylum and the world of the sane outside. Finally, true to the multidirectional, chaotic pattern, we are shifted simultaneously to the world of Watt in Knott's house, to his garden (but this is so imprecise that one may be forgiven if one assumes this is the garden of the asylum), and to the fantastic world of Arthur's Grants Committee. The end is, of course, foreordained. Watt somehow moves to the station after leaving Knott's house. Again we get a more or less concrete description of the station with various characters, but then Watt is waiting for a train which is supposed to take him where? Why, to the next cycle of the endless story.

Space calls, of course, attention to Time, its twin. But before we discuss this phenomenon we must turn to the question of language and Beckett's views on that subject.

Briefly, Vico held that human communication started in a prelingual state with mute signs and developed finally into the abstract generalizations of philosophy in an "inevitable progression." Thus it starts upward from dumb barbarians and reaches its final stage in corruption and decadence which is also a form of barbarianism or, as Vico calls it, the "barbarianism of reflection."[14] At this point, reflux sets in and we return once more to the beginning.

Vico, like his admiring disciple Beckett, devoted an enormous amount of discussion to the earliest stages of this progression which, as was noted before, corresponds to this historical cycle. Thus language in the first, theocratic stage, was sacred and expressed itself through the hieroglyph. The second or heroic stage corresponds to poetry or the metaphor. Those were the great stages of Greek mythology and poetry of which Homer is the brilliant example. (Vico, of course, concentrates on European or Western civilizations, paying no heed to Asia, Africa or the Western Hemisphere in the accepted mode of his day.) At any rate, what fascinated the young Beckett was this process which he called "the inevitable character of every progression or retrogression" and the possibility when the language had reached the final decadent stage and exhausted itself of its regeneration. One such technique used in revitalizing the language so that it approximates its earliest and vigorous stages is "direct expression." This, in Beckett's view, is exactly what Joyce had done in *Work in Progress*. Moreover this is what Dante has done in his *Divine Comedy*. Dante had taken an exhausted language which had broken down into regional dialects and constructed it anew. In fact, he had created a "synthetic language" which is entirely appropriate today as is demonstrated by the example of Joyce's work.

Two further observations must be made before we turn to the application of these linguistic conceptions to *Watt*.

The first concerns a special situation which Beckett does not touch upon in his essay on Joyce but which is briefly mentioned in a later "Verticalist Manifesto" concerning poetry which he co-signed along with various artists and writers. It appeared in 1932.

This concerns the term "mantic language." "Mantis" stems from the classical Greek where it means "seer." It is derived from "mainomai" which means to be in a frenzy or mad. Mantis was widely used (it appears in Homer) and seers, prophets or mediums were usually described as mad when uttering their truths, especially the oracle of Apollo at Delphi which Heraclitus describes. These truths were appropriately uttered partly in signs, partly in difficult language which only the wise could discern. At any rate, the various seers and oracles conveyed a message from the gods.

Although Vico does not use the term, he describes this particular form of communication as belonging to the Theocratic Age or sacred stage of his cycle and enthusiastically endorses it. It was in a way the language of the gods. To the Beckett of the "Verticalist Manifesto" of 1932 it was the language of a new poetry. Here is the pertinent quotation:

> The transcendental "I" with its multiple stratifications reaching back millions of years is related to the entire history of mankind, past and present, and is brought to the surface with the hallucinatory irruption of images in the dream, the daydream, the mystic-gnostic trance, and even the psychiatric condition.
>
> The final disintegration of the "I" in the creative act is made possible by the use of a language which is a *mantic instrument*, and which does not hesitate to adopt a revolutionary attitude toward word and syntax, going even so far as to invent a hermetic language, if necessary. [emphasis added] [15]

It might be noted parenthetically that one of the most famous exponents of the mantic concept at about the same time was the Swiss psychiatrist Carl Gustav Jung who, as we have shown before, had an indirect connection to Beckett. Jung held theories similar to Vico's and Dante's and called mantic writing "visionary."

The second situation concerns Beckett's discussion of Dante's language in another aspect of its revitalization. He praises it for using numbers symbolically. Vico, of course, devotes much analysis to the significance of numbers, sacred or otherwise, during the early stages of his historical cycles.

Kennedy has shown in great detail how all these concepts of language theories apply to *Murphy*. In a sense, they apply to all of Beckett's prose works—until he reached his own stage of exhaustion in the manipulation of his vision of a new language through direct expression and turned to drama.

Watt occupies a special position in this scheme of his development. Whereas in *Murphy* Beckett's conceptions regarding a "direct expression" or a "mantic" language are still underdeveloped, in a sort of Viconian gesture stage, while his reliance on symbolic numbers is extensive. In *Watt* a breakthrough has occurred. Numbers still are there but they are more decorative than vital. On the other hand, Beckett has developed his language to such an extent that it approaches his goal of "direct expression," although the ultimate aim still eludes him. "Form is content, content is form . . . This writing is not *about* something; *it is that something itself.*"16 This was his characterization of Joyce's work, but obviously it remained a mere ideal.

In Chapter I we examined verbal structures and linguistic structures. The emphasis was on individual words. We now turn to the other textual elements.

The most obvious aspect which strikes the reader is the peculiar arrangement of paragraphs and sentences which occurs throughout the novel whenever a situation of some impact occurs. The conventional paragraph structure has been abandoned for an endless flow of sentences. In fact, the sentences themselves, through a deliberate lack of punctuation, can be extended at times so that they run for a number of lines. This technique is used to portray rhetorical, descriptive and psychological states of the specific brand of rationalizing in the case of Watt when he indulges in speculations.

Two major structural patterns, vertical and horizontal, can be discerned.

Here is an excellent example of a horizontal pattern: It occurs during the hilarious examination of Louit by the Grants Committee.

> How extraordinary, I distinctly heard and seventy, said Mr de Baker. What did you hear, Mr MacStern? I heard and seven*teen*, with great distinctness, said Mr MacStern. Oh you did, did you, said Mr de Baker. The *n* is still ringing in my ears, said Mr MacStern. And you, Mr O'Meldon, said Mr de Baker? And I what? said Mr O'Meldon. Heard what, seven*teen* or seventy? said Mr de Baker. What did you hear, Mr de Baker? said Mr O'Meldon. And seventy, said Mr de Baker. And seven what? said Mr O'Meldon. And seven*teeeee*, said Mr de Baker. Naturally, said Mr O'Meldon. Ha, said Mr de Baker. I said and seventeen, said Louit. And seven what? said Mr Magershon . . . . [17]

Or a horizontal structure of a purely descriptive nature without dialogue:

> Here he stood. Here he sat. Here he knelt. Here he lay. Here he moved, to and fro, from the door to the window, from the window to the door; from the window to the door, from the door to the window; from the fire to the bed, from the bed to the fire; from the bed to the fire, from the fire to the bed; from the door to the fire, from the fire to the door; from the fire to the door, from the door to the fire; from the window to the bed . . . . [18]

An example of vertical textual structure:

> And the poor old lousy old earth, my earth and my father's and my mother's and my father's father's and my mother's mother's and my father's mother's and my mother's father's and my father's mother's father's and my mother's father's mother's and my father's mother's Mother's and . . . . [19]

The main function in a technical sense is expansion, even exaggeration in a certain direction. Technique bursts through conventional norms and becomes "direct expression." But what is accomplished by it is a heightened effect of various types.

If the first passage is examined we obtain the sense impact of a few old and half-deaf men squabbling over a trifle. Having stated it that way would be unsatisfactory to Beckett. Words like "squabble" or "trifle" or any other words that one could choose to describe this ridiculous scene could not convey the total impact. They are as exhausted as our language at large is. Therefore he constructs seemingly repetitive sentences which contain a carefully modulated structure of crescendo. In the second quotation, we obtain thus the picture of Knott restless and capable of moving in any direction at will, in fact through space almost like a god-like creature. In the third, human descent is vertically dramatized to show the expanse of time simultaneously. In each case a volume of words has been substituted for brevity.

These quoted passages, in spite of this interpretation, are not solely designed by Beckett for intellectual appreciation. Their impact is musical and their very repetitive tone recalls the ancient music of India and the Far East. At best, they are not only sheer sound-pleasing but also poetical. They obviously gain from being read aloud.

A major problem presents itself. It is all very well to speak of "exhausted" language which should be replaced by a new one. This is an idealized intellectual concept. How to execute it in reality is another matter. Beckett pointed to Dante and Joyce. The former, of course, wrote in Italian. Yet, surprisingly, Beckett deviated from Joyce's model as far as *Watt* is concerned.

There are several reasons for that, or what appear to be plausible reasons. In the first place there is the time element. While Beckett's point of view regarding the increasing exhaustion (and one might add vulgarization) of the English language has certainly been confirmed and reaffirmed in our own day, Joyce's experiments in *Finnegans Wake* did not turn out to be the hoped for solution. Certainly not by the time Beckett wrote *Murphy* and *Watt*. What looked persuasive in the 1920s and early 1930s did not look very practical by the late 30s and certainly not by the 1940s. Joyce's attempt to construct a new language, while shot through with genius, had resulted in an artificial creation which could be understood only by a tiny minority. Any literate Italian could easily read Dante but Joyce was reserved for mandarins. In other words, Dante had succeeded and Joyce had failed. This fact could not but impress Beckett who, besides, listened to the call of his own genius. The result is that we have in *Watt* not the dizzying Joycean gyrations and recreations of English but basically the English language intact. In fact, contemporary 20th-century English with a whiff of beautiful Irish lilt. Except for one aspect in which Beckett's view of "direct expression" is carried out. The verbal manipulation of heightening the sense impact through exaggeration and expansion.

Yet this *modus operandi* is too intellecutal, cerebral. It is imposed from above—or from the outside. It does not arise from the language medium naturally.

It has serious consequences as far as the characters in *Watt* are concerned. The technique is used almost exclusively by Arsene, Sam, Arthur and in a way by Watt as depicted by Sam. It is absent from the passages not attributable to Sam in which Watt appears. This, of course, is also true of the Dublin choruses who speak the cliché language of the day.

At any rate, the result is a confusion of narrators. In fact, a confusion of their points of view. In other words, given the differing character structures of Sam, Arthur, Arsene or Sam/Watt there is no reason why all of them should use that exaggerated form of communication. The fact that it is imposed on them from without shines through. Interestingly enough, Beckett grew apparently dissatisfied with the linguistic construction of endless sentences and struck out into differing directions in his later novels. Finally he abandoned his native language for French since apparently the English tongue, in his view, was not elastic enough.

Another linguistic process is present which seems more experimental, less a technical device, than a philosophical experiment in language which reflects Beckett's Viconian point of view. It is internal, part of the story of the novel and therefore organic. It is the

gradual deterioration of Watt's language, while in the mental insti-
sution, until Watt produces what Sam thinks are mere incomprehensible sounds. Sam has described for us this process, which is
mainly an inversion of words and sentence structure in great detail
which apparently went through the evolution of at least six stages
during the course of Watt's stay in the asylum. Interestingly enough,
when the climax of this decay has been reached, a mixture of sounds
and gibberish, Sam's hearing fails him—yet he "understands." What
he understands or how he understands we are not told. Presumbaly,
he understands the significance of Watt's language decay.

On one hand, as we have shown before, Watt's problem is
not unique. His inverted speech patterns do occur in schizophrenic
patients. So Beckett did not have to invent, knowledgeable as he was
about mental disease and mental hospitals. However, we can view
this process of language decay as the literary metaphor of an exhausted language. In other words, the super-rationalistic language of
the 20th century has reached the point where the "reflux" to barbarism has set in. The Viconian language cycle starts afresh with primitive sounds and gestures. This is the theocratic and sacred historical
stage where seers who are mad communicate the language of the gods
which is incomprehensible except to the few. The "mantic" language.

This interpretation sets up various possibilities. One we have
mentioned already: Watt no longer engages in his fruitless fatal speculations. He is turning into a simple—but healthy—barbarian. Of
course, he walks backward now, but this mirrors the entire backward movement, the reflux, of an exhausted rational Western civilization. Just as obviously he appears mad to the outside world—no
doctors or nurses appear in the asylum in contrast to *Murphy*, but
the outside world can be assumed to be the world of the conventional reader. If this is so, then the theories of the contemporary
British psychiatrist R. G. Laing may have been anticipated here.
Watt is not altogether mad. It is we who are mad or have driven
patients mad through certain insane practices in our society as suggested in *Murphy*.

On the other hand, if Watt is only half-mad but on the thresh-
hold of divine recognition, what does he see that we ordinary people
cannot discern? The ordinary people, not gifted with divine and mad
insight, are the people of the Dublin chorus at the end of the book.
They are concerned only with the immediate and surface appear-
ances. Watt, on the other hand, may have glimpsed in his divine madness the essence of an eternal cyclical process. He may have also
glimpsed its meaningless essence which is beyond time.

c) *The End of Western Rationality—from Descartes to Einstein and
    Heisenberg*

If the Wattian world mirrors the decline of the rational certainties of Cartesianism then it also mirrors the decline of Newton's
mechanics. Both have governed Western thought since the 16th
century and both collapsed in the beginning of the 20th. *"Cogito
ergo sum"* was overthrown along with Newton's celebrated concepts of "absolute space" and "absolute time." The latter were replaced by Einstein's "time-space continuum," the fourth dimension,
which indicated that time and space were not absoute but relative
while they posed alternatives even to the linear sanctities of Euclid-
ean geometry. Thus the universe itself might be spherical if not
elliptic. Even if it is not infinite, it might curve back on itself.[20]

These tremendous scientific developments with their atomic
by-products, Planck's Quantum theory and Heisenberg's "uncertainty" or "probability" principle as well as another Einsteinian discovery that energy equals mass have had some very interesting philosophical implications. This is Heisenberg's view:

> In the philosophy of Heraclitus of Ephesus the concept of Be-
> coming occupies the foremost place. He regarded that which moves,
> the fire, as the basic element. The difficulty, to reconcile the idea
> of one fundamental principle with the infinite variety of phenomena,
> is solved for him by recognizing that the strife of opposites is really
> a kind of harmony. For Heraclitus the world is at once one and
> many, it is just the 'opposite tension' of the opposites that consti-
> tutes the unity of the One . . . .

We may remark at this point that modern physics is in some way extremely near to the doctrines of Heraclitus. If we replace the word "fire" by the word "Energy" we can almost repeat his statements word for word from our modern point of view.[21]

If modern physics in the view of one of its greatest modern theoretical physicists is returning to the ancient doctrines of Heraclitus in many ways then this is stunning. Moreover, it appears Viconian. A cycle repeating itself. In other ways, it proves that the poet's intuition outdoes the laborious work of scientists. After all, Beckett sensed that trend without proving it by complex mathematical formulas. As for our specific subject, time, its plastic nature, so to speak, was also implicit in Heraclitus' views as well as those of other classic Greek thinkers.

In other words, in the extreme rationalism prevailing in the last three hundred years or so we assumed that time was absolute. Now we have reconsidered and found that it is relative, just as space, mass and energy are relative, doctrines which the ancient Greeks held.

In classical theory we assume that future and past are separated by an infinitely short time interval which we may call the present moment. In the theory of relativity we have learned that the situation is different; future and past are separated by a finite time interval the length of which depends on the distance from the observer. Any action can only be propagated by a velocity smaller than or equal to the velocity of light. Therefore, an observer can at a given instant neither know of nor influence any event at a distant point which takes place between two characteristic times.[22]

This explanation of the Einsteinian theory regarding the relativity of time governs all the physical actions in *Watt*. We can make this assertion confidently not only on the basis of the internal evidence but also because we know from many sources that Beckett was deeply read in modern scientific literatures, especially mathemetics, physics and astronomy, by the time he composed *Murphy* and *Watt*.

Let us take the simple example of Arsene's meeting with Ash on London's Westminster Bridge. Ash looks at a gunmetal "half hunter," announces the time is seventeen past five and rushes off. The next moment Big Ben strikes six. Arsene evaluates the scene as follows: "this in my opinion is the type of all information whatsoever, be it voluntary or solicited. If you want a stone, ask a turnover. If you want a turnover, ask plumpudding."24

After some remarks about Ash's subsequent death, Arsene launches into one of his great rhetorical sermons about his genealogy and the change of his seasons which demonstrate all is endless flux and change which constantly renews itself in time. It is also without meaning or purpose.

The scene with Ash and the different times on the two clock pieces is actually a metaphorical reworking of a celebrated section of Einstein's Special Theory of Relativity. There Einstein discusses the idea of "simultaneity" with reference to two clocks.

We do not have to elaborate on the intricate thought process involved here. We can easily see that Beckett has dramatized modern physical theory in the case of Ash and Arsene in somewhat crude and exaggerated but nevertheless effective terms. The only problem with the passage is that it may be misunderstood by readers who are not acquainted with Einstein or modern science. It could be dismissed as another one of Beckett's puns.

We can now attempt a more profound examination of Arsene's various attempts to dramatize the relativity of time for Watt. And once again we will find additional evidence why Watt will never understand. He is a hopeless and compulsive believer in the outdated world of Descartes and Newton. To him time, as it was to Newton, is absolute. This is self evident. His brain cannot allow any other possibility just as it cannot allow the possibility of non-Euclidian geometry. Besides, "Watt knew nothing about physics" anyway.

We can also understand now why Watt is constantly confused about time. First he cannot figure out the mysterious situation regarding Knott's rising and going to bed. Clearly, time seems "out of joint" here. Then he tries to figure out how long his service would last on the ground and first floors. This exercise gets him so confused that at the end he can only hear the croaking of frogs—which Beckett melodramatically dramatizes for us as an example of "direct expression." Finally time deserts him altogether. He despairs of ever working in Knott's floor and seeing his master. Then Arthur appears and suddenly we are transported into the garden of the asylum. We have, it appears, a new narrator in Sam—yet the story and the plot roll backwards and forwards at the same time. The expression "same time" is, of course, an illusion as are all the time elements in the novel. For, if time is indeed relative and dependent on the position of the observer, then an orderly, linear sequence of events which our conventionally-trained brains demand becomes impossible. In short, *Watt* as a novel—if our imperfect language medium could be replaced by mathematical formulas—could be read backwards. As a matter of fact, this process had already happened long before *Watt* was composed. Newton could fashion his theories of absolute time and space without using a single mathematical formula. At the beginning of the 20th century this was no longer possible. It is almost impossible to communicate by conventional language the full meaning of the formula $E=mc^2$. Energy equals mass times the square of the velocity of light is a verbal approximation, but this is nearly incomprehensible. Certainly, it cannot be grasped by our senses. Because, for one thing, we have no direct experience of it. Needless to say, Beckett knew all this.

Yet this knowledge reintroduces a familiar point of view. If language becomes exhausted under the impact and onrush of science, then perhaps science itself, or rather the complex science of today, labors under the fatal mark of decay.

Thus the character and all the other structures of the novel are not merely a reflection of relativity because that state is in itself an advance towards ultimate decay—and reflux. It might be noted here as regards to time that we find already in St. Augustine hints that an excessive preoccupation with it is a sign of the decline of a civilization.[25]

The only certainties left are change, flux, reflux, and the primary substance or principle, the One. According to Heraclitus it was fire. According to other Greek philosophers it was either water, or eternal motion. Heisenberg thinks Heraclitus' fire is close to today's concept of Energy. Whatever it may be, it bears an interesting resemblance to Knott who cannot be comprehended by Watt because he defies all rational laws. The "One" or "Unnameable" appears, of course, in Beckett's later novels.

Knott as a principle therefore does not exist in human form or with human attributes; he merely approximates them. Thanks to Beckett's art, Knott is made less nebulous. But Watt—or we—can never fully grasp him because he exists beyond time. Yet he fuels and propels all the characters around him as well as Watt. He moves forever in incomprehensible ways at incomprehensible speeds because he is energy which in turn is mass several times the speed of light in Einstein's formula.

Clearly, to portray such a force as Knott and the futile Wattian attempts to understand and fathom Knott in fiction—specifically through the medium of a language which Beckett regarded as exhausted—is more than a *tour de force.* It is a major accomplishment.

In fine, we can posit the following proposition: Beckett's usage of the Special and General Theory of Relativity, especially with respect to the time dimension in *Watt,* has widened its parameters. It has expanded its structures. It has released within the author new elements of imagination. In fact, imaginary possibilities which once were considered in the classic novel as "forbidden," chained as it was to the strictly linear and the causal. We may be initially disconcerted by the "illogical" time sequences, in fact, by the confusion between "beginning," "middle" and "end." Yet once we have accepted the flow of events this initial resistance melts away. In short, *Watt* has become more fictional and more real.

d) *The World as Illusion*

A few observers have pointed out traces of the influence of Eastern religions, Hinduism and Buddhism, in Beckett's later novels[26] and plays but these voices are few. Besides, no systematic study has been made. As for *Murphy* or *Watt* no such assertions have appeared.

In general the passivity, resignation and the meaninglessness of existence as it appears to these characters have been cited as testimonials of Eastern influence. Indeed, there is evidence of such levels in *Watt* as well. Apparently no one has noticed them. Other levels are represented or appear to be represented. Admittedly, we can only speculate here. Yet the parallels are striking and they cannot be omitted from any structural analysis of *Watt*. For their presence would not only reflect the point of view of the author and his created fictional characters but would add an ultimate structural dimension to the work.

The concept of the "meaningless" of various philosophical phenomena, such as life cycles, historical cycles or the process of change itself has been noted throughout this study, especially in quotations from Arsene's speech. Of course, Watt's speculations on one level could be construed as chasing after meanings, usually after the meanings of things or certain acts. Yet as was demonstrated before, this was only the surface level of the initial stage of the quality of Watt's intellectual games. Actually for Watt the hunt for meanings was not satisfactory. Neither was the hunt for hypotheses or solutions because they, too, supplied no answers. The excitement was only in the process of spinning speculations. As soon as a meaning, hypothesis or solution had been found he chased after others.

> So Watt did not know what had happened. He did not care, to do him justice, what had happened. But he felt the need to think that such and such a thing had happened then, the need to be able to say, when the scene began to unroll its consequences. Yes, I remember, that is what happened then.
>
> This need remained with Watt, this need not always satisfied during the greater part of his stay in Knott's house.[27]

In short, Watt hunted after meanings yet was indifferent to them. In the end of his stay he learned to accept. " . . . that nothing had happened, that a nothing had happened, learned to bear it and even, in a shy way, to like it. But then it was too late."[28]

This passage is very significant for it clearly suggests that Watt had been laboring under a grand illusion, composed of many illusions that created the many problems he thought existed and which he had to solve compulsively. On the other hand, it also suggests he has finally gotten a glimpse of a truth which has eluded him all his life, certainly during his stay in Knott's house: that his speculative pursuit was in vain, that he had been on the wrong path, a path which did not lead to liberation but to the enslavement of his senses, to madness. Yet this recognition, although too late in his existence, was in a way a part salvation.

Certain of these Beckettian ideas suggest Hinduistic and Buddhistic concepts. Both great religions, which are incredibly fragmented and exist in many schools, nevertheless have certain key factors which they incidentally share. (This is no coincidence because both were born in India and Buddhism sprang from Hinduism.)

The first outstanding characteristic is the possibility of personal liberation which in its ultimate stage, not accessible to everyone, results in finding a union with Brahman or Nirvana. Both are considered ultimate states which cannot be comprehended yet which confer bliss and happiness. The Hindu Brahman or the Buddhist Nirvana can be reached by various complicated stages. The decisive result of this ultimate liberation is the termination of the endless cycles of birth and rebirth or reincarnation which everyone undergoes. Hinduism more strongly emphasizes this than Buddhism. Everything, including the universe and its creator, Brahma (the representative of Brahman), is constantly created, destroyed and reborn according to fixed time cycles. Traditional Hinduism lists four ages or yugas, each of them 12,000 divine years in length. A divine year is equivalent to 360 human years. But one thousand of these yugas are merely a day for Brahma who himself lives only one hundred Brahma years and then is replaced by another Brahma. This upper limit of time is incomprehensible because time is infinite. However, there exist elaborate figures for sub-divisions and they have astronomical proportions. Nevertheless, it is obvious that we are encountering here some familiar concepts, especially the concept of cycles, of birth, decay, destruction and renewal and of ceaseless change.

Buddhism chooses a less "scientific" system. First, it assumes that nothing is permanent in empirical existence. Everything is subject to constant flux. All lives and rebirths are linked so that there is no break with the past which leads into the future. Ideally, a person could remember past existences. However, the focus of life is in the present which could be changed by practicing certain tenets. For instance, one of the first recognitions is to realize that life is full of suffering and to accept the phenomena of suffering.

In both religions there are strong suggestions not only of the impermanence of empirical phenomena and existence but of the external world. At the very least, these are distinguished from higher realities. At the extreme, such as in one school of Vedanta, the most prominent philosophical expression within Hinduism, the reality of the external world is denied altogether. The only reality is Brahma. All else is illusion.[29]

The very brief distillation suggests at once the "higher reality" of *Watt* which we can compare metaphorically to the tip of a spire or of a dome or pagoda. In the first place there are the cycles of the Hindu cosmology and its ages which are tantalizingly close to those of Vico, especially if one considers that the ages run from a golden age to one of decay and destruction when the cycle starts afresh. Incidentally, one great Irish literary figure who was heavily influenced by these cycles which he translated into his own conception of eras in a poetic manner was, of course, William Butler Yeats. One of the most notable poems in which he espoused his beliefs in "Leda and the Swan." More than that. Yeats helped to English some of the *Upanishads,* one of the major religious works of classical Hinduism. There can be no doubt whatever that Beckett was acquainted with it just as he was acquainted with Joyce's reading in those fields aside from his own philosophical and religious studies. So Beckett had two illustrious and influential Irish literary precursors in this respect.

The second aspect lies in the character structure of Watt. Granted that Watt is forever speculating in vain. Couldn't this very act of speculation be interpreted as search for liberation from his self to reach ultimate reality and bliss in the Hindu/Buddhist versions? True, we know all the catastrophic errors that his rationalistic thinking entails and commits. But this isn't typical modern Western thinking, a fact which even Arsene could only hint at but never quite articulate.

There are some strong hints that Watt *in extremis* may be using his intuition which is somewhat underdeveloped. Certainly the entire episode in Erskine's room when he discovers the painting and with it the circle suggests that he has found some higher meaning in a different way. He is tremendously moved in an emotional sense. It is clear that rationality plays no part in it. Those speculations are compulsive, without emotions, and in the end leave no impact on him. In fact, he does not care.

The character structures of Watt and Knott which eventually merge through synthesis suggest strongly, moveover, that in this union with Knott he has experienced something overwhelming. It is significant that all this occurs during his final stay in Knott's house when he is subject "to fancies" and his speculations have virtually stopped. Isn't it likely that Knott as the "basic principle" or the "One" also represents Brahma or Nirvana?

We can now understand, thanks to this analysis, what Sam eventually "understood" in Watt's sounds and gestures. Watt was trying to indicate through his god-like mantic sounds that he was reaching the highest levels of existence.

If this hypothesis is correct then Watt's ultimate literary structure is that of a pilgrim in search of salvation or liberation. His Western life does not permit him to follow the "right paths" of Buddhism or the more immediate approaches of Hinduism. He has to break down in order to do that. But seeing Watt as a pilgrim who travels about Dublin in very odd fashion, which outrages the citizenry, could be compared to the many figures wandering throughout most of Asia, certainly India, in search of a spiritual solution. There is an interesting similarity between these men and the figure of Watt. They are "odd" in the way Watt is (except that the Asian public does not consider them odd but respects them); they have abandoned the concerns and the forms, even the object of the external world as if it were illusory. What does it matter whether Watt wears two different size socks and shoes? If he were an Indian he would wear a loin cloth. Watt is not trying to impress the external world because it is of little importance to him. In fact, most of it may be an illusion.

If the external world is thus illusory, then the Watt of the final part of the novel is the pilgrim starting out on his search, the Western pilgrim to be specific, a search which is circular. Watt's search "ends" in the asylum—but Watt's existence is changed. He is reincarnated. The Watt we encounter, what in our terms is the "end" of the novel, is no longer the Watt of Knott's house. He is another Watt on a pilgrimage which begins anew, that is most likely to end for Western man in a mental breakdown as he strips off all the ways and illusions of our contemporary society.

Thus we return in circular fashion to a statement made at the beginning of this study. "There are many Watts among us." Many Watts searching for an escape of their self into a higher reality. This may well be the ultimate meaning of *Watt* as a novel.

Notes

[1]Leon Robin, *Greek Thought and the Origins of the Greek Spirit* (New York: Russell and Russell, 1967), pp. 73-74.

[2]*Ibid.,* p. 74.

[3]*Ibid.*

[4]Beckett, *Our Exagmination . . . ,* p. 5.

[5]*Ibid.,* p. 6. David Hayman in his essay, "*Molloy* or the Quest for Meaninglessness," in *Samuel Beckett Now* (Chicago: University of Chicago Press, 1970), p. 147, claims that this passage applies "to every line, every identity, every concept, analogy, character, image and book" of the trilogy of novels following *Watt.*

[6]Sighle Kennedy, *Murphy's Bed: A Study of Real Sources and Surreal Associations in Samuel Beckett's First Novel* (Lewisburg, Pa.: Bucknell University Press, 1971), *et. passim.*

[7]*Watt*, p. 44.

[8]Werner Heisenberg, *Physics and Philosophy, The Revolution in Modern Science* (New York: Harper Torchbooks, 1958), pp. 76-92.

[9]*Our Exagmination . . .* , p. 5.

[10]Benedetto Croce, *The Philosophy of Giambattista Vico* (New York: Russell and Russell, 1964), p. 122.

[11]Kennedy, *Murphy's Bed,* p. 36.

[12]*Our Exagmination . . .* , p. 7.

[13]*Ibid.,* p. 22.

[14]Croce, *The Philosophy of Giambattista Vico,* p. 212.

[15]*Murphy's Bed,* p. 304.

[16]*Our Exagmination . . .* , p. 14.

[17]*Watt,* p. 185.

[18]*Watt,* pp. 203-204.

[19]*Watt,* p. 46.

[20]*Heisenberg,* pp. 125-126.

[21]*Ibid.,* pp. 62-63.

[22]*Ibid.,* p. 115.

[23]Kennedy, *et. passim.*

[24]*Watt,* p. 46.

[25]*The Basic Writings of St. Augustine: The Confessions* (New York: Random House, 1948), vol. I, book XI. The entire section on the meaning of

Time is of course expressed in Christian religious terms, but it has many points of convergence with modern scientific theories.

[26]*Hayman,* p. 148.

[27]*Watt,* p. 74.

[28]*Watt,* p. 80.

[29]This abstraction is based on Vernon McCasland, Grace Cairns and David C. Yu, *Religions of the World* (New York, 1969), *A Source Book in Indian Philosophy,* ed. Sarvepalli Radhakrishnan and Charles A. Moore (Princeton: Princeton University Press, 1957), and other volumes cited in the general bibliography.

Chapter V

Conclusion

The history of the Western novel in the 20th century is primarily the history of the experimental novel. However, in retrospect it appears persuasive that the composition of *Watt* in 1944-45 was a landmark in this respect. Beckett at that point of his career had deserted the tutorial umbrella of his master James Joyce. He left the Epic/Archaeological/Linguistic experiment which had so preoccupied Joyce and established his own direction. Propelled by his special bent for the philosophical and the scientific, especially the mathematical, Beckett's new orientation found first fruit in *Murphy* and was followed by the flowering of *Watt.*

The artistic conception of these novels differs radically. *Murphy,* in spite of its heavy emphasis on astronomy, astrology, mathematics and certain philosophical concepts, is essentially a conventional novel with easily discernible plot, characters, setting, even thematic content. Time sequences are linear. Spatial relationships are not obscured. Characters are individualized even though a mystic element is introduced by the use of astrology. We know that Murphy is somewhere in London, that his friends are searching for him, that he finally obtains a position in a mental hospital and we know how his life is ended. The relationships of the other characters are sometimes a bit obscured, but in the main we are presented with a coherent picture of how they react. Thus from the standpoint of plotting the novel presents no great difficulties. It is at times chaotic, but the machinery of its plot structures generally keeps diversive elements under control and moves the story towards its appointed end.

We still do not know why Beckett arrived at the remarkable complexities and mysteries of *Watt* as a novel. But we do know, or at least we have tried to show, the influences that shaped its artistic conception. Some of them were of long standing, especially those behind the ideas that he expressed in his essay in 1929 on Vico, Bruno and Dante with respect to philosophy and language.

These influences can be summarized briefly. The attraction of opposites or identified contraries *à la* Bruno, Vico's cyclical theory of the decay, reflux and rebirth of history and language, Dante's "reordering" of the chaotic Italian language and the structure of the "Divine Comedy," all flavored strongly by the Heraclitian tenets of eternal primordial flux. The element of language decay, or to put it precisely, of Beckett's native English language, may be said to have developed in stages. The concept of language decay and rebirth was already present, as we have seen in 1929. Yet Beckett later committed himself more strongly by signing the so-called Verticalist Manifesto of 1932 with its emphasis on language as a "mantic instrument" which would revolutionize words and syntax. Such a position would lead to the disintegration of the "I" in the creative act. This position was a major step away from Joyce who was still mired, so to speak, in the re-creation of an Ur-epic.

Other influences, of course, impacted on a maturing Beckett, mostly of a scientific nature. Contemporary science was transforming the world or at least its presupposed stability and found a willing listener in Beckett who had considerable mathematical gifts. Yet Beckett, while utilizing scientific tools at the same time saw the danger. Western science was propelled forward by a Cartesian reasoning which ultimately threatened to destroy the personality. The mystic East, which did not rely on purely logical reasoning in its philosophies, had proceeded differently. Its religious philosophies contained a strong ingredient of intuition. In fact, Vico had characterized philosophy or philosophical thinking as a sign of a very advanced civilization in decay.[1]

Yet all such concepts do not a novel make. Yet Beckett appears to have approached his task of transforming or incorporating such concepts into a novel with some trepidity. True, strong traces are already evident in *Murphy,* even though Beckett's ideas had not yet quite matured.

A dramatic event must have brought this creative act about. The conclusion is inescapable that Beckett's artistic spark was kindled by the shattering events of the Second World War. He experienced it first hand. He was living like the embryo Watt not only in its madhouse but like a hermit in the center of the hurricane.

Consider, for instance, the following situation: An Irish intellectual named Samuel Beckett is hiding out in a remote Provençal village. Technically, as an Irish citizen, he is a neutral. Yet at the same time he is being hunted as an enemy by the German occupation authorities. During daylight hours he ekes out a bare subsistence posing as a French farmhand (aided by his remarkable knowledge of the French language). Thus this individual leads simultaneously four existences. Which one is the real Beckett? It is easy to say that the real Beckett is the Anglo/Irish novelist. Yet the other three Becketts not only existed simultaneously, they can be even documented. Which one is Beckett's "I"? Is he a harmless teacher or a secret resistance worker? And how do the different worlds perceive him? Where lay the ultimate truth about this man? This period of Beckett's multi-faceted, multiple existence offers a fertile field for further research, certainly in a psycho-literary/historical sense.

Beckett's real-life situation during the writing of *Watt* is a perfect example of the disintegration of the "I"—or at least its fragmentation—which is one of the key structural elements of *Watt*. For in that novel Beckett eliminated many elements hallowed by tradition and convention. Obviously, he overthrew the clearly defined character and he replaced him with a multi-dimensional character who exists simultaneously in various dimensions of time and space. In short, not only are such characters composed of a multiplicity of character traits which themselves exist independently on various levels, but also, the structures (as well as their substructures) approach each other, oppose, then combine and eventually transform in an unending process.[2]

If a novel contains such beings which seem to float through space, setting and time independent of the traditional novelistic laws then the entire structure of the novel changes. "Chaotic," conventional critics call it.

Our conslusion suggests the contrary. We have attempted to demonstrate that the whole of the novelistic structure is controlled. Not strictly controlled, to be sure. But controlled in the sense that Beckett allowed the story to develop with a certain degree of plasticity. In other words, instead of a clearly-defined plot, non-linear plot elements exist simultaneously. Absolute time elements are replaced by relative time. Spatial relationships melt and blur. Scenes dissolve into each other without chronological and logical sequence. Our highly structured Apollonian consciousness demands order while Beckett is actually presenting us with Dionysian revels. However, it is not to be implied—as so many critics have asserted—that this disorder is a deliberate attempt on Beckett's part to satirize the outmoded "well-made" novel by creating an "anti-novel."

On the contrary, there is a very serious purpose underneath the playful confusion. Beckett's aim in this respect is to portray the formlessness, the chaos of life, without using traditional rules which appear to him as artificial. In other words, for Beckett, content becomes form and content equals form.

The technique used in this respect approximates the science of cinematography whose compositional film techniques ("close-up," "fade-out," "cuts," and "montage") enable the director's camera to depict characters in a three-dimensional setting, especially in flashbacks when the minds of the characters return to former scenes within their experience. *Watt* is filled with flashbacks which sometimes occur quite abruptly without any preparation. An entire generation of French writers who developed the "nouveau roman" in the 1950s and 60s were to follow the same cinematographic tendencies in this respect. Alain Robbe-Grillet and Michel Butor are good examples.

However, the adoption of this technique by French writers later on represented a certain trend. As it turned out, the "nouveau roman" with its existentialist stance and "anti-hero" almost assumed a simplistic ideological vogue which was shunned by Beckett's *Watt* or his trilogy that followed it. In fact, Beckett's conception of a novel implicitly expressed in *Watt,* is unique. The translation of its metaphysical, philosophical, aesthetic, and linguistic concepts into art was extremely difficult and impossible to duplicate. Even for Beckett. One can infer this by considering the sharp break that followed in his development as a novelist.

Watt's verbal, character, and plot structures are unique, and reinforced by formidable scholarship and learning. Just as the plot follows simultaneously circular and linear progressions which can be clearly traced, so the verbal structures follow certain precepts wholly wedded to the universe of the novel. These structures compose characters whose qualities, development, interactions, and actions are uniquely suited to a situation in a time frame in which such people as Watt, Arthur, Knott, Arsene, Hackett, Mrs. Gorman, and the rest exist—an Irish setting existing sometime during the first part of the 20th century. True, the characters may symbolize certain cosmological, ontological, and metaphysical verities which Beckett uses as underpinnings to build his thematic superstructure, but Beckett also succeeds in adopting the characters to a specific human setting and tailoring the structural apparatus supporting it. Beckett has not tried to incarn in his people a host of ancient symbols *à la* Joyce. There is no Anna Livia Plurabelle here. Watt is not Ulysses, Achilles or Isaiah. Watt is a modern man, in the sense that he is a victim of the tendencies of rationalistic thinking that has prevailed in the West since Descartes. He possesses a well-defined personality in this respect. He lacks the iron will of the conqueror and, more importantly, he lacks the artistic temperament and intuition which would free him from the treadmill of fruitless speculations. Besides, he lacks humor. As we noted in our analysis, he is not only an intellectual *manqué* but he represents a very definite and ubiquitous type in our urban society. To wit, the half-baked scholar-clerk with his compulsions and illusions who often goes mad or becomes merely "neurotic."

One cannot speak of a theme in this novel as if it were a unified single concept with a chic shingle labelled "exile," "alienation," "metaphysical *angst*," or "the horror of the human condition." The concept of a single theme, as is found in more conventional novels is as alien to *Watt* as the character of Watt is alien to the world of the Dubliners. Instead, Beckett has given us a panoply of thematic conceptions ranging from the deadly character mixture of superrationalism mingled with irrational fantasies, so representative of the contemporary human Watt type, to highly abstract philosophical conceptions about the nature of the universe. On the other hand, *Watt* relates the simple story of a man who has a certain problem which lands him in an insane asylum. All the numerous thematic delicacies are spread on a table before the reader like a smorgasbord. One can choose and pick as in real life. Some persons are confused by the rich spread. Others pick a few pieces they recognize. A few are dazzled by the magnificence yet perceptive enough to appreciate the master's touch which has composed the spread in the first place. They immerse themselves in an endless feast.

In addition to the array of themes indissolubly linked with philosophical conceptions relayed to us by various mysterious narrators, thematic scraps are embedded in such odd places as songs or in *bons mots* in the so-called "addenda" to *Watt* which function like clarifying notes. Arsene whose long "briefing" of Watt in the form of a monologue contains a major portion of Beckettian philosophy is an exception. His speech is filled with solid thematic and philosophical chunks.

Unfortunately Beckett has not made it easy for us to select the thematic dishes. His intellecutal equation of content and form has not only overthrown the orderly sequence of the conventional novel but employed a novel and complex approach to what is usually termed "point of view." Naturally, these innovations have proved to be highly confusing and mysterious to many students and have led to endless, sometimes silly, interpretations.

While the intellectual concept of shifting narrators is a highly valid one in a theoretical sense, it hovers close to failure in an artistic dimension. And the scattering, fragmentation, and fusion of narrators, themes, points of view, and intellectual concepts is our failure as well. By approaching *Watt* rationally we tend to slip into the trap that eventually undoes Watt. For we demand clear statements, precise narration expressed by well-defined narrators, concise situations in an artificial literary sense. Yet none exist in that fashion because none exist in real life. By thus approaching *Watt* we deny the ur-instinct which had been so suppressed in Watt that it had ceased to operate.

The reader must approach *Watt* intuitively, like a poem or like a religious fragment, and absorb its complex essences. The nuggets of truth are there in *Watt*, but they are embedded in the dross of life without pattern or scheme and are frequently invisible. One must experience *Watt* in a mantic state before interpreting it. The rational interpretation should never be considered absolute. Nothing is absolute in life since everything is relative and in flux. Beckett seems to mock us with the statement that "if you think such and such an idea is in *Watt*, then it is there."

It is highly pertinent therefore that Beckett has been inhospitable to requests for an "explanation" of his work. For to explain what it "means" would be to violate his own artistic credo.[3]

In regard to the problem of Beckett's linguistic experiments, the author tried in *Watt* to revive a language that to him appeared to be exhausted just as the novel form had become exhausted. This laudable attempt was not successful as discussed earlier even though, theoretically, it nearly succeeded.

Beckett encountered the same type of failure in the narrative and thematic structure which, on one hand, attempt to give us a truer picture of life, stripped of the false artifices of the conventional novel. Their virtue lies in their elevating the novel to a greater "literarity" and "fiction" by striking out, equipped with a revivified language, into previously unknown zones. Yet, in doing so, such narrative and linguistic tenchiques place an intolerable burden on the reader, and produce an ironic result. While more "fictional" in a theoretical sense, *Watt* becomes more "literary" in a practical sense. For the average novel reader it becomes a closed book, a fate which has befallen many experimental non-conventional novels of our time. Quite evidently Beckett in his succeeding novels changed course and eventually found the right groove for his genius in the drama. It is no coincidence that he succeeded in the dramatic form without changing his philosophical concepts.

At this point we can now answer a question posed in Chapter IV. Why didn't Beckett write a philosophical treatise on Watt?

He introduces a formidable array of scholarship in *Watt* and he also displays intellectual positions which are the fruit of years of meditation. He had previously exhibited a brilliant discursive style in his essay "Dante . . . Bruno. Vico . . . Joyce" and in his critical study of Marcel Proust. There is little question that he could have handled the materials which formed *Watt* successfully in a critical/ philosophical study which would have also included his aesthetic views regarding fiction. After all, the material of *Watt* is readymade for such treatment.

One does not have to delve into the mysteries of Beckett's psyche to find the answer. With the exception of *Murphy* and the aforementioned two studies, his work prior to *Watt* consisted essentially of poetry and some playlets. (He also translated a number of essays from the French but that was not original work.) His natural and most powerful inclination was to create fiction yet he obviously felt after *Murphy* that the ingredients of a path-breaking novel would also have to include a new philosophical basis as well as a new language.

He must have realized that this attempt was artistically only a partial success. Certain modifications had to be made in his novelistic approach. The most immediate change was effected by transforming his language, a process John Fletcher has analyzed very well in his study of Beckett's novels.[4]

The overall implications of *Watt* are complex. Any summary of them must include the attempt to overthrow the structure of the conventional novel, the reorganization of conventional language and the introduction of contemporary scientific principles which led to intricate structural complexities, multidimensional characters, a relativity of chronology, spatial relations and of the narrative process itself—all designed to present a truer picture of human existence. In other words, to equate the chaos and dissonances of life with the form and content of the novel. The philosophical ingredients, so important in *Watt*, are nevertheless secondary as far as the implications for the contemporary novel as a whole are concerned. In the first place, philosophical ingredients have always been present in the novel and, in the second place, any number of philosophical concepts could have been used. The other ingredients of *Watt* were of greater significance. Many have been used in the contemporary experimental novels with varying success, and they have been refined and expanded. Thus *Watt* blazed a trail.

Obviously, the last word has not been spoken regarding *Watt*. In addition to a number of areas suggested earlier in our analysis of *Watt* which deserve further investigation, we see a rich field of study inherent as well in the relationship between *Watt* and *Mercier and Camier,* language and the musical elements in *Watt,* the structural elements in *Watt* as compared to those of the "Trilogy" (with emphasis on English versus French language patterns), and Beckett's religious and political beliefs during the era which saw the composition of *Watt*. Other topics for further study will undoubtedly suggest themselves to the reader of *Watt,* for its varied richness offers no end to the speculation that has centered and will center upon it.

Notes

[1]John Fletcher, *The Novels of Samuel Beckett* (New York: Barnes & Noble, 1964), pp. 245-247, lists a number of French articles dealing with various aspects of the black experience which Beckett translated during the 1930s. This phase of Beckett's development is highly interesting and deserves further investigation.

[2]Beckett has finally managed to eliminate characters altogether in his recently published work, *The Lost Ones* (New York: Grove Press, 1972). This novel was begun in 1966 and first published in French as *Le Dépeupleur* (Paris: Editions de Minuit, 1971). It is essentially a short scientific/philosophical tale.

[3]See Beckett's reply to Sighle Kennedy's inquiry, *op. cit.,* pp. 300-302.

[4]Fletcher, *Novels,* pp. 90-110.

Bibliography

A Source Book in Indian Philosophy. Ed. Sarvepalli Radhakrishan and Charles A. Moore. Princeton: Princeton University Press, 1957.

Abbott, Porter. *Form and Effect.* Berkeley and Los Angeles: University of California Press, 1973.

Albert Einstein Philosopher-Scientist. Ed. Paul Arthur Schilpp. New York: Tudor Publishing Co., 1951.

Approaches to Poetics. Ed. Seymour Chatman. New York: Columbia University Press, 1973.

Bardsley, Charles W. *English Surnames; Their Sources and Significations.* 1st ed. 1889. rpt. Rutland, Vt.: E. E. Tuttle Co., 1968.

Barnard, G. C. *Samuel Beckett: A New Approach. A Study of the Novels and Plays.* New York: Dodd, Mead & Company, Inc., 1970.

Barthes, Roland. "Alain Robbe-Grillet." *Evergreen Review,* II (5 1958), pp. 113-26.

—. *Critical Essays.* Evanston, Ill.: Northwestern University Press, 1972.

—. *Mythologies.* New York: Hill and Wang, 1973.

—. *S/Z.* New York: Hill and Wang, 1974.

—. *Writing Degree Zero.* Boston: Beacon Press, 1970.

Beckett, Samuel. "Dante . . . Bruno. Vico . . . Joyce." *Our Exagmination Round his Factification for Incamination of Work in Progress.* Paris: Shakespeare and Co., 1929.

—. "Anna Livia Plurabelle." *Nouvelle Revue Française* (May 1931), pp. 637-46.

—. *Endgame.* New York: Grove Press, 1958.

—. *Krapp's Last Tape and Other Dramatic Pieces.* New York: Grove Press, 1960.

—. *Malone Dies.* New York: Grove Press, 1956.

—. *Mercier and Camier.* New York: Grove Press, 1974.

—. *Molloy.* New York: Grove Press, 1955.

—. *Murphy.* New York: Grove Press, 1957.

—. *Proust.* London: Chatte and Windus, 1931.

—. *The Lost Ones.* New York: Grove Press, 1972.

—. *The Unnameable.* New York: Grove Press, 1958.

—. *Waiting for Godot.* New York: Grove Press, 1954.

—. *Watt.* New York: Grove Press, 1959.

—. *Three Dialogues: Samuel Beckett and Georges Duthuit.* London: John Calder, 1965.

—, J. Putnam and Georges Duthuit. *Bram van Velde.* New York: Grove Press, 1960.

Beckett at 60: A Festschrift. London: Calder and Boyars, 1967.

Bernal, Olga. *Langage et fiction dans le roman de Beckett.* Paris: Gallimard, 1969.

Blanchot, Maurice. "Where Now? Who Now? *Evergreen Review* 2 (Winter 1959), pp. 222-29.

Booth, Wayne C. *The Rhetoric of Fiction.* Chicago: University of Chicago Press, 1961.

Brooke-Rose, Christine. "Samuel Beckett and the Anti-Novel." *London Magazine* (Dec. 1958), pp. 38-46.

Bruno, Geordano. *The Expulsion of the Triumphant Beast.* Trans. and Ed. Arthur D. Imert. New Brunswick, N. J.: Rutgers University Press, 1964.

Bruns, Gerald L. *Modern Poetry and the Idea of Language.* New Haven: Yale University Press, 1974.

Chatman, Seymour. *Literary Style: A Symposium.* New York: Oxford University Press, 1971.

Coe, Richard. *Samuel Beckett.* New York: Grove Press, 1964.

Cohn, Ruby. "A Note on Beckett, Dante and Geulincx." *Comparative Literature 12* (Winter 1960), pp. 93-94.

—. *Samuel Beckett: The Comic Gamut.* New Brunswick, N. J.: Rutgers University Press, 1962.

—. "Still Novel." *Yale French Studies* (Summer 1959), pp. 48-53.

—. "Watt in the Light of The Castle." *Comparative Literature 13* (Spring 1961), pp. 154-66.

Contemporary Novels: Six Introductory Essays in Modern Fiction. Ed. William O. S. Sutherland. Austin: University of Texas Press, 1962.

Croce, Benedetto. *The Philosophy of Giambattista Vico.* New York: Russell and Russell, 1964.

Culler, Jonathan. *Structuralist Poetics.* London: Routledge and Kegan Paul, 1973.

Deleuze, Gilles. *Proust and Signs.* New York: George Braziller, 1972.

Driver, Tom F. "Beckett by the Madeleine." *Columbia University Forum 4* (Summer 1961), pp. 21-25 [Interview]

Duhamel, Albert and Richard Hughes. *Literature: Form and Function.* Englewood Cliffs, N. J.: Prentice-Hall, 1965.

Ellman, Richard. *James Joyce.* New York: Oxford University Press, 1959.

Esslin, Martin, ed. *Samuel Beckett: A Collection of Critical Essays.* Englewood Cliffs, N.J.: Prentice-Hall, 1965.

Federman, Raymond. *Journey to Chaos: Samuel Beckett's Early Fiction.* Los Angeles: University of California Press, 1965.

Fletcher, John. "Samuel Beckett and the Philosophers." *Comparative Literature 17* (Winter 1965), pp. 43-56.

—. *Samuel Beckett's Art.* New York: Barnes & Noble, 1967.

—. *The Novels, of Samuel Beckett.* New York: Barnes & Noble, 1964.

Friedman, Melvin J. "A Note on Leibniz and Samuel Beckett." *Romance Notes 4* (Spring 1963), pp. 93-96.

—. "The Novels of Samuel Beckett: An Amalgam of Joyce and Proust." *Comparative Literature 12* (Winter 1960), pp. 47-58.

—. "Samuel Beckett and the Nouveau Roman." *Wisconsin Studies in Contemporary Literature I* (Spring/Summer 1960), pp. 22-36.

Frye, Northrop. *Anatomy of Criticism: Four Essays.* Princeton: Princeton University Press, 1957.

Garvin, Paul L. *A Prague School Reader on Esthetics, Literary Structure and Style.* Washington, D. C.: Georgetown University Press, 1964.

Genette, Gérard. *Figures.* Paris: Seuil, 1966.

—. *Figures II.* Paris: Seuil, 1969.

—. *Figures III.* Paris: Seuil, 1972.

Gessner, Niklaus. *Die Unzulanglishkeit der Sprache: eine Untersuchung uber Formzerfall and Beziehungslosigkeit bei Samuel Beckett.* Zurich: Juris-Verlag, 1957.

Gras, Vernon W. *European Literary Theory and Practice: From Existensial Phenomenology to Structuralism.* New York: Delta Books, 1973.

Guillen, Claudio. *Literature as System.* Princeton: Princeton University Press, 1971.

Harvey, Lawrence. *Samuel Beckett—Poet and Critic.* Princeton: Princeton University Press, 1970.

Hassan, Ihab. *The Literature of Silence: Henry Miller and Samuel Beckett.* New York: Alfred A. Knopf, 1967.

Heisenberg, Werner. *Physics and Philosophy—The Revolution in Modern Science.* New York: Harper Torchbooks, 1958.

Hesla, David H. *The Shape of Chaos: An Interpretation of the Art of Samuel Beckett.* Minneapolis: University of Minnesota Press, 1971.

Hoefer, Jacqueline. "Watt." *Perspective II* (Autumn 1959), pp. 62-76.

Hoffman, Frederick J. *Samuel Beckett: The Language of Self.* Carbondale, Ill.: Southern Illinois Press, 1962.

Humphries, Christmas. *An Invitation to the Buddhist Way of Life for Western Readers.* New York: Schocken Books, 1969.

—. *The Wisdom of Buddhism.* New York: Random House, 1961.

Introduction to Structuralism. Ed. Michael Lane. New York: Harper & Row, 1972.

Jacobsen, Josephine and William Mueller. *The Testament of Samuel Beckett* New York: Hill and Wang, 1964.

Jameson, Frederic. *The Prison-House of Language.* Princeton: Princeton University Press, 1972.

Joyce, James. *Finnegans Wake.* New York: Random House, 1976.

—. *Letters.* 3 vols. Ed. Stuart Gilbert. New York: Viking Press, 1966.

—. *Ulysses.* New York: Random House, 1934.

Kennedy, Sighle. *Murphy's Bed: A Study of Real Sources and Surreal Associations in Samuel Beckett's First Novel.* Lewisburg, Pa.: Bucknell University Press, 1971.

Kenner, Hugh. *A Reader's Guide to Samuel Beckett.* New York: Farrar, Straus and Giroux, 1973.

—. *Samuel Beckett: A Critical Study.* New York: Grove Press, 1961.

Laing, R. D. *The Divided Self.* London; Penguin Books, 1965.

Le Sage, Laurent. *The French New Novel.* University Park, Pa.: Pennsylvania State Universtiy Press, 1962.

Lévi-Strauss, Claude. *The Savage Mind.* Chicago: University of Chicago Press, 1966.

—. *Totemism.* Boston: Beacon Press, 1963.

Manhattan Directory. New York Telephone Co., 1976-7.

Marissel, André. *Samuel Beckett.* Paris: Editions Universitaires, 1967.

Matejka, Ladislav and Krystyna Pomorska. *Readings in Russian Poetics.* Cambridge: MIT Press, 1971.

Matthews, C. M. *English Surnames.* New York: Scribner's, 1967.

Mauriac, Claude. *The New Literature.* Trans. Samuel I. Stone. New York: George Braziller, 1959.

McCasland, S. Vernon, Grace Cairns and David C. Yu. *Religions of the World.* New York: Random House, 1969.

Mercier, Vivian. "The Mathematical Limit." *The Nation* (Feb. 14, 1959), pp. 144-45.

Moorjani, Angela B. "Narrative Game Strategies in Bekcett's *Watt.*" *L'Esprit Créateur XVII, 3* (Fall 1977), pp. 235-44.

Nadeu, Maurice. "Samuel Beckett, l'humour et le néant." *Mercure de France* (August 1951), pp. 693-97.

New French Writing. Ed. Georges Borchardt. New York: Grove Press, 1961.

Peierls, R. E. *The Law of Nature.* New York: Chas. Scribner's Sons, 1956.

Piaget, Jean. *Structuralism.* Trans. and Ed. Chaninah Maschler. New York: Basic Books, 1970.

Pritchett, V. S. "An Irish Oblomov." *New Statesman* (April 2, 1960), p. 489.

Relativity Theory: Its Origins and Impact on Modern Thought. Ed. L. Pearce Williams. New York: John Wiley, 1968.

Roberts, Edgar V. *Writing Themes about Literature.* Englewood Cliffs, N. J.: Prentice-Hall, 1969.

Robin, Leon. *Greek Thought and the Origins of the Scientific Spirit.* New York: Russell and Russell, 1967.

Samuel Beckett Now: Critical Approaches to His Novels, Poetry and Plays. Ed. Melvin J. Friedman. Chicago and London: University of Chicago Press, 1970.

Samuel Beckett: A Collection of Critical Essays. Ed. Martin Esslin. Englewood Cliffs, N. J.: Prentice-Hall, 1965.

Saussure, Ferdinand de. *Course in General Linguistics.* New York: McGraw-Hill, 1966.

Scholes, Robert. *Structuralism in Literature.* New Haven: Yale University Press, 1974.

—   and Robert Kellogg. *The Nature of Narrative.* New York: Oxford University Press, 1966.

Scott, Nathan A. *Samuel Beckett.* New York: Hillary House, 1965.

Shklovsky, Victor. *Sur la theorie de la prose.* Lausanne: L'age d'homme, 1973.

Stroup, Herbert. *Four Religions of Asia: A Primer.* New York: Harper and Row, 1968.

—.   *Like a Great River; An Introduction to Hinduism.* New York: Harper and Row, 1972.

Structuralism: An Introduction. Ed. David Robey. Oxford: Clarendon Press, 1973.

Sypher, Wylie. *Loss of the Self in Modern Literature and Art.* New York: Random House, 1962.

Szanto, George H. *Narrative Consciousness: Structure and Perception in the Fiction of Kafka, Beckett and Robbe-Grillet.* Austin: University of Texas Press, 1972.

The Basic Writings of St. Augustine. 2 vols. Ed. Whitney J. Oates. New York: Random House, 1948.

The Dialogues of Plato. 2 vols. Trans. B. Jewett. New York: Random House, 1937.

The Language of Criticism and the Sciences of Man. Ed. Richard Macksey and Eugenio Donato. Baltimore: Johns Hopkins University Press, 1970.

The New Science of Giambattista Vico. Trans. Thomas G. Bergin and Max H. Fisch. Ithaca, N. Y.: Cornell University Press, 1968.

Tindall, William York. "Beckett's Bums." *Critique 2* (Spring/Summer 1958), pp. 3-15.

—. *Samuel Beckett.* New York: Columbia University Press, 1964.

Todorov, Tzvetan. *Introduction à la littérature fantastique.* Paris: Seuil, 1970.

—. *Poétique de la prose.* Paris: Seuil, 1965.

—. *Théorie de la littérature.* Paris: Seuil, 1965.

Uspensky, Boris. *A Poetics of Composition.* Berkeley: University of California Press, 1973.

Wahrhaft, Sidney. "Threne and Theme in Watt." *Wisconsin Studies in Contemporary Literature 4* (Autumn 1963), pp. 261-78.

Wizsacker von, C. F. and J. Juilfs. *The Rise of Modern Physics.* Trans. A. J. Plmerans. New York: Braziller, 1957.

Wellek, René. *The Literary Theory and Aesthetics of the Prague School.* Ann Arbor: University of Michigan Press, 1969.

Yeats, William Butler. *The Collected Poems.* New York: The Macmillan Company, 1949.